MYLES MUNROE

DAILY DEVOTIONAL JOURNAL
A 40-Day Personal Journey

REDISCOVERING THE
KINGDOM

ANCIENT HOPE
FOR OUR
21ST CENTURY WORLD

Text compiled by Jan Sherman

Destiny Image® Publishers, Inc.
P.O. Box 310
Shippensburg, PA 17257-0310

"Speaking to the Purposes of God for This Generation
and for the Generations to Come"

ISBN 0-7684-2296-5

For Worldwide Distribution
Printed in the U.S.A.

This book and all other Destiny Image, Revival Press, MercyPlace, Fresh Bread, Destiny Image Fiction, and Treasure House books are available at Christian bookstores and distributors worldwide.

1 2 3 4 5 6 7 8 9 10 / 11 10 09 08 07 06 05

To place a book order, call
1-800-722-6774.

For more information on foreign distributors, call
717-532-3040.

Or reach us on the Internet:
www.destinyimage.com

TABLE OF CONTENTS

DAY 1

DISCOVERING THE ORIGIN AND PURPOSE OF MAN

THEN THE KING WILL SAY TO THOSE ON HIS RIGHT, "COME, YOU WHO ARE BLESSED BY MY FATHER; TAKE YOUR INHERITANCE, THE KINGDOM PREPARED FOR YOU SINCE THE CREATION OF THE WORLD."

(MATTHEW 25:34)

TODAY'S DEVOTION

It is not unreasonable to ask why God, the King of heaven, would want to create sons in His image and a visible universe. Was He not satisfied and pleased with an invisible realm of angels and powers to rule? I believe the answer to these questions lies in understanding the very nature of God Himself. There is much about this great awesome, self-sustaining One that we do not, cannot, and may never know, but He has revealed enough of Himself to mankind to allow us to glimpse some of the magnificence of His nature and character.

One such characteristic is that "God is love" (1 John 4:8,16)....It is this inherent nature of love that motivated the King of heaven to create spirit children (called mankind) to share His Kingdom rulership. In other words, man was created for the purpose of rulership and leadership. This is why in the message of Jesus, when He described the age of the Kingdom of God and its provision for man, His indication was that this Kingdom belonged to man before earth was created....

It was God's idea to share His invisible Kingdom with His offspring, which He called mankind, and give to them His nature and characteristics.

(Quote From *Rediscovering the Kingdom*, Pages 25-26)

QUESTIONS

1. It was God's desire to create sons in His image. What parts of His image do you see in mankind? How have you been created in God's image? Do people easily see the image of God in you?

2. As you look at the nature of God, describe five of His attributes that directly deal with man. In regards to each of these five, tell why you appreciate them and how they have been demonstrated in your life.

3, How did love cause God to create us? How did love cause God to create you? Are you aware of His love toward you? Have you received it deeply, or is God's love difficult to grab hold of?

4. If God wants us to share in His rulership, how should man prepare himself for such a role? How do you gain the necessary tools and instruction to rule effectively? Is rulership something that comes "natural" to you?

5. Describe the borders of the Kingdom of God. Where does the Kingdom begin and end? How do its boundaries define where and who come under your rulership?

MEDITATION

"Man is the crowning act of an intentional Creator.
He exists as God's co-regent in a world created for him"
(*Rediscovering the Kingdom*, Page 24).

This quote is packed with meaning. Meditate
on each phrase as you discern its meaning
for mankind and their impact on your life.
- *Crowning act*
- *Intentional Creator*
- *God's co-regent*
- *World created for him*

THE BIRTH OF THE KINGDOM—THE SPIRIT OF DOMINION

THEN GOD SAID, "LET US MAKE MAN IN OUR IMAGE, IN OUR LIKENESS, AND LET THEM RULE OVER THE FISH OF THE SEA AND THE BIRDS OF THE AIR, OVER THE LIVESTOCK, OVER ALL THE EARTH, AND OVER ALL THE CREATURES THAT MOVE ALONG THE GROUND." SO GOD CREATED MAN IN HIS OWN IMAGE, IN THE IMAGE OF GOD HE CREATED HIM; MALE AND FEMALE HE CREATED THEM.

(GENESIS 1:26–27)

Man was created to exercise power and designed to manage it. The motivating purpose for the creation of the human species was to dominate the earth and its resources, the result of the Creator's desires to extend His rulership from the supernatural realm to the physical realm. His plan and program was to do this through a family of spirit children He would call His sons. The record of this creative act is found in Genesis 1:26....

This statement is the first declaration of God's intent for you and me, and encompasses the total purpose, assignment, potential, passion and design of man as an entity. This statement is the key to man's natural desires, sense of purpose and fulfillment in life. There are a number of critical principles imbedded in this first mission statement of God, concerning man's creation, that must be carefully examined:

1. Man was both *created* and *made*....

2. Man was made in God's image....

3. God created man....

4. The Creator said let "them" have dominion over the earth....

5. Let them have dominion....

6. Over the fish of the sea, the birds of the air, the livestock, earth, and all that creep upon the ground.

(Quote From *Rediscovering the Kingdom*, Pages 27-30)

QUESTIONS

1. Examine each of the six principles above. Find a Scripture to support each one.

2. Rewrite each of the six sentences or phrases in your own words so that an unbeliever would understand each principle.

3. Regarding each of the principles, give an example from your own life that speaks to their truth. Personalize these as your testimony.

4. Considering each of these principles, do you live as though you really believe them to be true? Why or why not?

5. Choose one of the six principles to pray into your daily life, in terms of your attitude, responses, decisions, and actions.

MEDITATION

*"**To be given dominion means to be established as a sovereign, kingly ruler, master, governor, responsible for reigning over a designated territory, with the inherent authority to represent and embody as a symbol, the territory, resources and all that constitutes that kingdom.** This definition should be memorized, understood and embraced by the spirit of every man if we are to understand the original purpose and will of God our Creator for our existence"*

(Rediscovering the Kingdom, Page 31).

So, do it!

A KINGDOM PROMISED

And I will put enmity between you and the woman, and between your offspring and hers; He will crush your head, and you will strike His heel." To the woman He said, "I will greatly increase your pains in childbearing; with pain you will give birth to children. Your desire will be for your husband, and he will rule over you.

(GENESIS 3:15–16)

The loss of the Kingdom of heaven on earth was considered rebellion against the eternal imperial Kingdom of heaven and the creating of a vagabond state. Earth became a territory under an illegal government. While Adam committed high treason, the instigator and adversary, the evil one, executed an earthly coup....Adam did not lose heaven when he fell; rather, he lost...legal representation of heaven on earth....

However, God's most significant response to this defection and treacherous act was His promise to the adversary recorded in Genesis 3:15-16....

The heart of this promise is the coming of an "offspring" through a woman who would break the power of the adversary over mankind and regain the authority and dominion Adam once held, and through a process of conflict, restore the Kingdom back to mankind. This was the first promise of a messiah-king and the return of the Kingdom. Therefore, the greatest need of mankind was identified by what he lost; he did not lose a religion or heaven, but rather a kingdom. In God's restoration and redemptive program, heaven would not be His primary focus or goal for man, but rather the redemption, restoration and re-establishment of His kingdom on earth. This would be the principle purpose and assignment of the promised Messiah....

Adam lost the kingdom. The consequences of this rebellion were numerous:

- Loss of position and disposition;
- Transfer of responsibility;
- Self-consciousness and shame;
- Fear and intimidation of authority;
- The loss of domination over nature;
- Frustrated toil and hatred of labor;
- Pain and discomfort; and,
- The need for human accountability.

(Quote From *Rediscovering the Kingdom*, Pages 34-35)

1. What are some ways that humanity has continued to bear the consequences of Adam's rebellion?

2. Have you borne the consequences of Adam's rebellion personally? In what ways?

3. Search for scriptural promises or answers for each of the consequences listed above.

4. Using the list you wrote for #3, determine which promises you have applied to your life in order to change your consequences into possibilities.

5. Which of the consequences seems to plague you the most? Memorize the Scripture you chose that refers to that consequence. Begin to apply it today.

MEDITATION

"God knew before time began that we would
never find Him without His help. Therefore, God
launched a journey. He set out to find us. God is the
chaser and we are the pursued. Instead of allowing us
to expend our lives in continual frustration trying to reach
up and touch Him, He came down to take hold of us. His
desire and purpose were to bring us back into relationship
with Himself and return to us the lost Kingdom"

(Rediscovering the Kingdom, Page 36).

How does it feel to be pursued by God?
Do you allow Him to catch you? What should happen
when He does? Take time to pray and let this happen.

DAY 4

SONS OR SERVANTS

Now a slave has no permanent place in the family, but a son belongs to it forever. So if the Son sets you free, you will be free indeed.

(JOHN 8:35-36)

A closer look at God's original plan will reveal how great a divide exists between religion and relationship. God originally intended to extend His heavenly Kingdom on earth through mankind. In this plan, *God's purpose was to establish a family of sons, not a household of servants.* Just as Scripture shows us that men are Christ's Bride, so, too, are women God's sons. In Christ we are all heirs (see Rom. 8:14)....Jesus makes a clear distinction between servants and sons....

Jesus said that sons are members of the family, but servants are not. From the beginning, God wanted offspring who would relate to Him in love, not slaves or "hired hands" who would obey Him out of obligation. Servants may relate to their master on a superficial level, but no intimacy or sense of family exists. Sons, on the other hand, are part of the family; they are heirs who will inherit everything that belongs to their father.

God's purpose was to establish a Kingdom of sons, not subjects....God is indeed a King, but He does not want subjects. He wants sons. He does not want to rule us, but to have a family who shares His rulership.

(Quote From *Rediscovering the Kingdom*, Pages 39-40)

QUESTIONS

1. Reflect upon the original purpose and plan God had for mankind. How has the history of man demonstrated the following? How has mankind lived opposite to their purpose?

   • Establish a family of spirit sons, not servants.

   • Establish a Kingdom, not a religious organization.

   • Establish a Kingdom of kings, not subjects.

   • Establish a commonwealth of citizens, not religious members.

   • Establish relationship with man, not a religion.

   • Extend His heavenly government to earth.

   • Influence earth from heaven through mankind.

2. Find verses, parables, or stories in Scripture that reflect each of the purposes listed above.

3. How can the future of man find its original purpose again? What posture will the Church need to take? What will Christians need to believe?

4. What will be needed to bring your life into alignment with the original purpose and plan of God? Is there a first step that you might take?

5. Set up a prayer schedule when you will pray for each purpose that is iterated above.

MEDITATION

*"God's Kingdom is different from earthly kingdoms in that it has no subjects. There are no peasants in the Kingdom of God, only sons. In the Kingdom of God we are not subjects but members of the royal family....Everyone in God's Kingdom is a prince or princess. There are no peasants or middle class, and no order of servants. In God's Kingdom, **everyone** is related to the King"*

(*Rediscovering the Kingdom*, Page 40).

How should the concept of being part of "The Royal Family" affect your attitude toward your successes? Your defeats?

RULING THE VISIBLE WORLD FROM THE INVISIBLE REALM

B Y FAITH WE UNDERSTAND THAT THE WORLDS WERE PREPARED BY THE WORD OF GOD, SO THAT WHAT IS SEEN WAS NOT MADE OUT OF THINGS WHICH ARE VISIBLE.

(HEBREWS 11:3 NAS)

God's simple strategy for extending and establishing His Kingdom on this earth was to rule the visible world of man from the invisible realm of the spirit. The plan meant that man would be His visible representative created specifically to live in the visible realm to represent Him....

How would He accomplish this? God, who is unseen, would put His Spirit into the unseen spirit of man—a spirit inhabiting a visible physical body living on the visible earth. Through man's spirit a window of the soul is created so that man can communicate with the invisible world of God and also through another window man is able to communicate through his body to the visible world of man. Man is created in such a powerful and unique way that he is exalted above all of God's creation.

By this means God could communicate from the unseen realm through the unseen spirit man to the seen realm, so that the visible world of man could understand His will. Whatever God desired would be relayed to the unseen, then manifested in the seen on the scene so that the earth would show what heaven was thinking.

(Quote From *Rediscovering the Kingdom,* Pages 43-44)

QUESTIONS

1. Why do you think God chose to rule the visible world of man from the invisible realm of the spirit? How does this strategy help extend and establish the Kingdom on earth?

2. How well do you represent God on earth? What is your reputation among believers? Unbelievers? Does your presence make a difference wherever you go? *yes! GOD goes w/me*

3. How does man communicate with the invisible world of God? Think about how you have experienced this communication. What took place?

4. How does God communicate through the bodies of His representatives to the visible world of man? Are there different ways the communication comes to the Church than to the world?

5. Why is it so important that man understands the will of God? Is it possible for His will to be understood in the government sector? Business sector? Family? Church? Community? How might this happen?

MEDITATION

"Right or wrong, most unbelievers have a definite
idea of what they think a Christian should be. If we
are not careful, we can identify too strongly with
their label and fall into the trap of trying to live up
to their expectations. We should stop trying so hard
to live like **Christians** and all of the false assumptions
associated with that term, and instead work harder at
living like sons and daughters of God, brothers and
sisters of Christ, and citizens of the Kingdom of heaven"

(Rediscovering the Kingdom, Page 42).

Think about the trap of trying to live up to unbelievers'
expectations. Have you fallen into that trap? How will
you live more like a son or daughter in the future?

the sincere
First I was drank Milk of Word of God
a Baby & then a
child
grows
up,
teenager = SON
and
NOW
Becoming
a F. &
Son

Father
DO HIS WILL + Keep his WORD. + ACT.

JESUS
By His Holy Spirit leading Me, Guiding
Feeding me, Teaching Me +
I following HIM + his instruction.

A KINGDOM OF KINGS

G OD BLESSED THEM AND SAID TO THEM, "BE FRUITFUL
AND INCREASE IN NUMBER; FILL THE EARTH AND
SUBDUE IT. RULE OVER THE FISH OF THE SEA AND THE
BIRDS OF THE AIR AND OVER EVERY LIVING CREATURE
THAT MOVES ON THE GROUND." = BUG's (GENESIS 1:28)

you may not come in this house! iUN
I say so! so Get Out! NOW!

Notice also that [this] verse say[s] nothing of human beings ruling over other human beings. It was not God's original design that any man would rule other human beings. *He created all of us to rule, not to be ruled.* In accordance with His own plan, God needed someone to dominate a piece of real estate called earth, so He created man. God made us to be in charge of this unique territory, to rule over the earth domain. Many of us have either lost sight of this truth or never learned it in the first place. Understanding that we were created for dominion carries truly life-changing ramifications.

God's purposes never change. He remains committed to His plan for man to dominate this planet on His behalf. Trapped inside every one of us is a dominion spirit crying for release and a dominion mandate waiting to be exercised. It is this natural spirit of dominion that causes us to naturally rebel against any attempt to dominate or control our lives or destiny. [That is why we go crazy whenever we are under someone else's domination.] Whether the oppression comes from religion or the world systems, humans were not meant to live a life of subjugation and will always resist oppression.

(Quote From *Rediscovering the Kingdom*, Page 46)

QUESTIONS

1. Describe the extent of our rulership on earth. What does it include? What is not under our realm of rulership? Why?

2. If God "created all of us to rule, not to be ruled," how do you explain systems of government where there are rulers and citizens? How do courts and judges fit into these systems?

3. Why do you think many of mankind lost sight of the fact that God charged us to dominate earth? What might have happened if we had kept this within our sight?

4. What are some of the ramifications Christians will experience when they begin to understand their dominion on earth? How might your life change if you increase your dominion over the earth?

5. Why does man "naturally rebel against any attempt to dominate or control" their lives? What factors are at work in this rebellion? Is this rebellion intrinsically good or evil? Explain your answer.

Elohim,

"At creation, God gave man dominion over
the entire physical realm, making him the de facto
king of the earth. To **dominate** means 'to govern, = H.S.
rule, control, manage, lead, or have authority over
something.' There is a very important distinction here.
God gave us **rulership** of the earth, not ownership.
Someone who gives up ownership to another person
also surrenders all responsibility for it. The person
who assigns the position of rulership of a place but
retains ownership, will retain the ultimate responsibility"

(Rediscovering the Kingdom, Page 48).

Based on these concepts, what is God's responsibility
to the earth? What is your personal responsibility?

We just will be Blessing Together & Loving

A Legacy for all our Children To Follow in Our Foot Steps • as we Follow Holy Spirit

STAY close to GOD On an Intimate Way • For us all!

In the Jim Mullane Family = PRAY + STAY
I as his Queen am To Pray for all
of us To make Heaven + shun Hell and
that Our H.H. Father's Will get's done! =
Pray; Thank, Praise + Worship God for us all "Making it".
Back to Our Heavenly Home Because of Jesus' Grace
and His Mercy! (You + your Household shall Be Saved.
I will Building an ARK for all of us who
I am

BORN TO RULE,
NOT TO BE RULED

May the Lord make you increase, both you and your children. May you be blessed by the Lord, the Maker of heaven and earth. The highest heavens belong to the Lord, but the earth He has given to man. (Psalm 115:14–16)

Get Left Behind!

We were born to rule the earth—all of us. When we do not become who we were meant to be or fulfill our destiny, we open the door to a whole world of personal problems. Allowing ourselves to be dominated by our physical environment or by other people can result in things like high blood pressure and other physical problems and illnesses. It can even open the door to mental and emotional troubles.... Psalm 115 states it perfectly....

Verse 16 is an awesome verse. The phrase "the highest heavens" refers to the heavens above the stratosphere—the invisible world where God lives. Heaven is God's realm, but He gave the earth to man, not in a deed of ownership, but as a lease agreement of proprietorship. Here the Bible tells us directly that heaven is not our territory.

Believers often talk about going to heaven when they die. Although that is true, God has made arrangements to make sure that we don't stay there. If we stayed in heaven, God's Word would fail, because He has plainly stated that He created us to have dominion over the earth. God's Word can never fail....

(Quote From *Rediscovering the Kingdom,* Page 49)

QUESTIONS

1. When we do not fulfill our destiny to rule the earth, what types of problems invade the world? What types of personal problems come as a result?

2. What is the difference between a deed of ownership and a lease agreement of proprietorship? How does the lease agreement best describe our earthly position?

3. Describe what you think heaven is like. How does God's rulership enter into your picture? What aspects of His rulership do you think we will enjoy?

4. What does the author mean when he says that God does not mean for us to stay in heaven? How does this concept challenge the popular ideas of what our "hereafter" is like?

5. What plans does God have for us to rule earth? What kind of earth do you think we will rule? What kind of life might it be?

MEDITATION

*"God is and remains absolutely sovereign,
but He has chosen to limit His activity or
intervention on the earth to that which we,
the proprietors, give Him permission to do. The
way we grant that permission is through prayer"*
(*Rediscovering the Kingdom*, Page 51).

*Why did God choose to limit His activity on earth
to what we permit Him to do? What is your part of
the responsibility order that will invoke His activity?*

BUILDING A KINGDOM MENTALITY

THEREFORE, I URGE YOU, BROTHERS, IN VIEW OF GOD'S MERCY, TO OFFER YOUR BODIES AS LIVING SACRIFICES, HOLY AND PLEASING TO GOD—THIS IS YOUR SPIRITUAL ACT OF WORSHIP. DO NOT CONFORM ANY LONGER TO THE PATTERN OF THIS WORLD, BUT BE TRANSFORMED BY THE RENEWING OF YOUR MIND. THEN YOU WILL BE ABLE TO TEST AND APPROVE WHAT GOD'S WILL IS—HIS GOOD, PLEASING AND PERFECT WILL.

(ROMANS 12:1-2)

It all comes down to whether or not we have a *Kingdom mentality*. If you believe that you are supposed to follow all the time, then follow on; the world is full of people who will be more than happy to lead you. If, however, you detect the seed of leadership in you, if you see evidence of the dominion mandate in your spirit and commit yourself to follow it, nothing can stop you. That mandate is inside every one of us, for God put it there....

As children of God and sinners saved by the blood of Jesus, we have no reason to feel ashamed of who we are or to sell ourselves short. Instead, we should embrace our identity as beings created in the image of God. We are like our Father, and we should live accordingly, boldly claiming our rights as citizens of a heavenly Kingdom....

God gave us dominion over the earth, an awesome responsibility as well as a wonderful privilege. Let us not conduct ourselves like vagabonds, servants, or hired hands who have no personal interest or stake in the land, but as wise children giving careful and confident management of a realm that we stand to inherit one day.

(Quote From *Rediscovering the Kingdom,* Pages 55-56)

QUESTIONS

1. Describe what you think is a "Kingdom mentality."

2. Rate yourself on the following aspects of the Kingdom mentality:
   - Detecting the seed of leadership in yourself.

   - Seeing evidence of the dominion mandate in your spirit.

   - Committing yourself to follow your mandate.

3. Find Scriptures or illustrations in the Word that (a) describe people having a Kingdom mentality, and (b) give directives regarding each of the above aspects.

4. Choose one of the three aspects of Kingdom mentality to concentrate on during your prayer time. How will you need to change your thinking to embrace it?

5. Does management of the earth confine itself to the environment and nature? What are others areas it might also include?

MEDITATION

"Paul says next that we need to 'be transformed
by the renewing of [our] mind.'…His point is that
even though as believers we have been born again,
we still have a mental problem. We have the Holy
*Spirit, but not the **spirit** of the Holy Spirit. We*
*have the anointing but not the **spirit** of the*
anointing. We need to change our thinking.…
The transformation that Paul talks about here
involves a complete revolution of our mental state"

(*Rediscovering the Kingdom*, Page 59).

What "mental problem" do you have
in regard to the Holy Spirit and the
anointing? How must your thinking change?

REDISCOVERING THE KINGDOM CONCEPT

But seek His kingdom, and these things will be given to you as well. Do not be afraid, little flock, for your Father has been pleased to give you the kingdom.
(LUKE 12:31-32)

❧ TODAY'S DEVOTION ❧

I t is most important to note that God the Creator chose the concept of a kingdom to communicate His purpose, will and plan for mankind and earth to us. The message of the Bible is primarily and obviously about a Kingdom. If you do not understand kingdoms, it is impossible for you to understand the Bible and its message.

However, over the past 2,000 years the true concept of kingdom has been lost, especially since the advent of modern governments built on new concepts of governing, e.g., democracy, socialism, communism, and dictatorships....

The kingdom concept was born in the heart of man, placed there by his Creator as the purpose for which he was created. Despite the fact that there were many types of kingdoms throughout history, there are certain characteristics common to all kingdoms. The Kingdom of God, according to Jesus, also possesses these components....

All kingdoms have:
- A King and Lord – a sovereign;
- A Territory – a domain;
- A Constitution – a royal covenant;
- A Citizenry – community of subjects;
- Law – acceptable principles;
- Privileges – rights and benefits;
- A Code of Ethics – acceptable lifestyle and conduct;
- An Army – security; and,
- A Commonwealth – economic security; and,
- A Social Culture – protocol and procedures.

(Quote From *Rediscovering the Kingdom*, Pages 63-64)

QUESTIONS

1. If we have handled our call to dominion so poorly, why is the Father so pleased to give us the Kingdom? (See Luke 12:31-32.)

2. Defining the kingdom concept through the characteristics common to all kingdoms can be useful as you explain the Kingdom of God to unbelievers. For each bulleted item above, name the Kingdom component defined.

3. Proof of each of these components above is found in Scripture. Find a verse or passage for each one that contains the component and the identity of who or what each is.

4. Of the components listed above, determine what responsibility you have to make a difference, if any. Is there anything you can do to help the component take its proper place in the earth today?

5. Understanding the components of the Kingdom of God can help you see your daily actions as conducting Kingdom business. What business will God expect you to attend to today as you conduct business on earth? From what perspective will you need to view the circumstances of the hours before you?

MEDITATION

"Religion has...diverted our understanding by converting the message of the Kingdom of God into a moral belief system. The result is that religion has become an end in itself, distinguishing itself from the Kingdom concept with pride. In fact, many religions take pride in the separation of religion and state and see the two as opposing entities with no common relationship. The dilemma is that the Kingdom is a state government with all the characteristics of a state" (Rediscovering the Kingdom, Page 63).

What is your answer to those who speak about separation of church and state? How is the Kingdom of God different from a moral belief system? What are you able to do to allow the Kingdom to invade earth in a practical way?

KINGDOM COMPONENTS

I WILL MAKE YOU INTO A GREAT NATION AND I WILL BLESS YOU; I WILL MAKE YOUR NAME GREAT, AND YOU WILL BE A BLESSING. I WILL BLESS THOSE WHO BLESS YOU, AND WHO- EVER CURSES YOU I WILL CURSE; AND ALL PEOPLES ON EARTH WILL BE BLESSED THROUGH YOU.   (GENESIS 12:2-3)

TODAY'S DEVOTION

All kingdoms are comprised of a number of components necessary for them to function effectively. All kingdoms, including the Kingdom of God, have:

- A Health program – healing;
- An Education program – Teaching ministry of the Holy Spirit;
- A Taxation system – Tithing;
- A central Communication system – Gifts of the Spirit;
- A Diplomatic Corps - Ambassadors of Christ;
- A System of Administration – the Ministration of the Spirit through mankind called the Church; and,
- An Economy – a system of Giving and Receiving (seed time and harvest time).

A careful study of the biblical message and the presentation of the message of the Kingdom of heaven by Jesus will illustrate the presence of all these components and characteristics of life in the Kingdom of God.

However, the most outstanding element distinguishing the Kingdom of God from every other kingdom is the concept that *all* of its citizens are relatives of the King, and are kings themselves. This was the message brought to earth by the Lord Jesus Christ....

This declaration was known as "the promise" and activated the long historical expectation of a Messiah king destined to redeem all men and restore them back to their kingly position.

(Quote From *Rediscovering the Kingdom*, Pages 67-68, 70)

QUESTIONS

1. Defining the kingdom concept through the programs common to all kingdoms is important as you gain a biblical worldview. For each bulleted item above, name an example of a specific Kingdom program.

2. Proof of each of these programs above is found in Scripture. Find a verse or passage for each one that contains the program and an example of that program.

3. Of the programs listed above, determine what responsibility you have to make a difference, if any. Is there anything you can do to help the program take its proper place in your community?

4. Understanding the programs of the Kingdom of God can help you plan your priorities of family, work, and ministry. How should your day planner reflect these priorities?

5. If *all* citizens of the Kingdom of God are relatives of the King, what responsibilities do they bear? If *all* citizens of the Kingdom of God are kings themselves, what authority do they share?

MEDITATION

"The divine strategy was the return of the
original Adam to earth to reconstruct the old
Adam that had failed. The means would be the
coming of the Messiah King to redeem, restore and
reconnect man back to heaven's government once again.
This promise of a royal seed in Genesis 3:15 established
the coming of God in the flesh as a legal redeemer with
all the rights to enter earth's realm to achieve this goal"
(Rediscovering the Kingdom, Page 70).

From what specific things has Christ
redeemed you? In what state is your restoration?
Do you feel connected to heaven's government?

IMAGE OF A KING

THEN THE SOVEREIGNTY, POWER AND GREATNESS OF THE KINGDOMS UNDER THE WHOLE HEAVEN WILL BE HANDED OVER TO THE SAINTS, THE PEOPLE OF THE MOST HIGH. HIS KINGDOM WILL BE AN EVERLASTING KINGDOM, AND ALL RULERS WILL WORSHIP AND OBEY HIM.

(DANIEL 7:27)

Caesar issued coins stamped with his image and inscription. People understood that whatever bore Caesar's image belonged to Caesar and he had every right to claim it. Likewise, they could understand that whatever bore God's image and stamp of ownership belonged to God and was His for the claiming. When we come to Jesus and give Him our lives, the first thing He does is change our name. He gives us His name and calls us His sons and daughters. John tells us that to those who believe in His name He gives the right to become children of God (see John 1:12). As children of God, we are joined together with Christ and seated with Him on His throne in heaven next to our Father.

The Bible says that as believers we are citizens of heaven. That remains true no matter where we go. Whenever I travel internationally, I carry my passport with me, which identifies me as a Bahamian citizen to every foreign official who needs to see it....Likewise, we do not have to be *in* heaven to be citizens there. Right now, we live on earth, but are citizens and ambassadors of the heavenly Kingdom, which is our true home.

(Quote From *Rediscovering the Kingdom*, Pages 77-78)

QUESTIONS

1. When people look at you, do they see that you bear the stamp of ownership, indicating to everyone that you belong to God? Just as a coin bears an inscription, what would you suggest be "inscribed" on your face to let others know who owns you?

2. In what ways do you bear the image of God? In outward appearance? In inward beauty? In words? In actions? Other?

3. Considering that God changes your name when you come to Him, does your earthly name have more significance or the name of your Father? Which one should bear the most weight? Why?

4. The author tells us that we are joined together with Christ. What does this mean to you?

5. The author also tells us that we *are* seated with Christ on His throne in heaven next to our Father. These words indicate present tense and do not refer to the future after our death. What does this mean to you? How is this possible?

MEDITATION

*"The Roman senate was called the **ecclesia**,*
a Greek word that means 'assembly,' or 'called-out
ones.' Greek and Latin were both widely spoken
throughout the Empire. Jesus spoke Aramaic, the
common language of the Jews of Palestine, but the
Gospels were originally written in Greek. The Gospel
*writers use the word **ecclesia** in passages where Jesus*
talks about building His 'Church.' Just as Caesar had
an assembly of called-out ones—the Senate—so also did
Jesus Christ, the Son of the living God and King of
kings, have His assembly of called-out ones—His Church"
(*Rediscovering the Kingdom*, Page 77).

Describe your local church representative
of the "called-out ones" in terms of its
demographics, its importance to the community,
and its differences compared to the world culture.

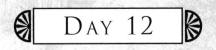

THE SEEDS
OF LEADERSHIP

Y OU HAVE MADE THEM TO BE A KINGDOM AND PRIESTS
TO SERVE OUR GOD, AND THEY WILL REIGN ON THE
EARTH. (REVELATION 5:10)

When God created us, He gave us everything we need to fulfill His original plan and purpose. Because God designed us to lead, the seeds of leadership lie within us, dormant until they are ready to be activated by the power of God. For this reason, leadership is not something we should have to *study* as much as something that is already inside us. It is a matter of discovering and nurturing those powers of leadership within us.

Within the earthly realm, God has given us great freedom. Ultimately, the kind of leaders we become and the degree of dominion we exercise depends upon us. God will never violate our freedom or override the dominion spirit He placed within us. Although, I must say that He might make life awfully unbearable for us until we turn toward Him. The Holy Spirit will never force our hand. But as we allow Him, the Holy Spirit will convict us, guide us, and lead us, but He will never *drive* us....

As Creator, God knows what is inside each one of us because He put it there. Whenever God speaks to you, He addresses you based on what He knows about you, not on what other people think they know.

(Quote From *Rediscovering the Kingdom*, Page 81)

QUESTIONS

1. What or whom do you lead? Is it generally easy for you to lead, or is it difficult? Are there certain areas where it is more difficult than others? Why?

2. As you consider the seeds of leadership that have been placed within you by God, trace these seeds through your life, developing a timeline. How has your leadership been developed? How do you think the Lord will continue to school you in the ways of leadership in the immediate future?

3. God's Kingdom is full of leaders. Do you think too many leaders in any kingdom can bring chaos? Are there any followers? How can Kingdom business flow with a Kingdom full of leaders?

4. Have you experienced times when leading and taking dominion seemed impossible? What did you do? Did you find the faith to override your fears and doubts, or did you succumb to them? How might we grow in leadership and dominion for future challenges?

MEDITATION

"Some of you may question this concept
of the leadership potential within you. Maybe
you consider yourself to be a follower and not a leader.
Maybe you think you don't have the skills, qualities,
ability, or experience to be a leader. Perhaps you have
accepted the negative things others have said about you.
In truth, it does not matter what other people say
or think, or even what we think of ourselves. What matters
is how God sees us, and He sees us as leaders and rulers
in the earthly domain. He created us for this purpose and
designed us with the necessary abilities to fulfill our destiny"

(*Rediscovering the Kingdom*, Page 81).

Do you feel like a leader? Are there areas
in your life where you would rather be a
follower? What makes you want to take a
backseat when God is asking you to lead forward?

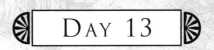

KNOWLEDGE: INFORMATION FROM GOD

To the Jews who had believed Him, Jesus said, "If you hold to My teaching, you are really My disciples. Then you will know the truth, and the truth will set you free."

(JOHN 8:31-32)

The first thing God gave Adam for their protection was information: "You are free to eat from any tree in the garden; but you must not eat from the tree of the knowledge of good and evil, for when you eat of it you will surely die" (Gen. 2:16-17)....As long as they obeyed God and respected His boundaries, they would live and prosper and enjoy unlimited fellowship with their Creator....

Knowledge lies at the heart of the struggle between the two kingdoms, because knowledge is where the adversary mounted his original attack on humanity. Satan's most powerful weapon is ignorance, but to use it he must first destroy or distort true knowledge. That is exactly what he did with Adam and Eve in the Garden of Eden. He deceived and overcame them by attacking the source and substance of their knowledge....

As a result of satan's ploy, Adam and Eve developed a distorted understanding of the knowledge God had given them. They succumbed to the devil's manipulation and trickery to become "like God," although *they were already like Him*....In their sin, Adam and Eve, rather than becoming like God, they became less like God than they were before.

(Quote From *Rediscovering the Kingdom,* Pages 86-87)

QUESTIONS

1. How does information afford us protection? Are we responsible for the information we have received? Is there any excuse for not using that knowledge?

2. Obedience is key to life, prosperity, and enjoying unlimited fellowship with our Creator. Why is obedience so important?

3. Why does God give us boundaries when we are supposed to be rulers? Does each boundary limit our realm? Why or why not?

4. Has satan ever distorted knowledge that you received from God so that you were tempted to sin? How can we tell the difference between truth and deceit?

5. How were Adam and Eve already like God from the very beginning? In what ways did they become less like God when they ate from the tree?

MEDITATION

"In a practical sense, from the beachhead
established at Calvary, we must move forth
in an all-out attack to free mankind from bondage
to the devil and his evil kingdom of darkness. We who
are in Christ must work to eliminate the ignorance
of those still trapped in the darkness of satan's
deceptions. The antidote to ignorance is knowledge.
Knowledge comes through truth, and truth brings liberation"
(*Rediscovering the Kingdom*, Pages 85-86).

Who are the people around you who are
trapped in the darkness of satan's deceptions? How might
you bring them knowledge, truth, and therefore, liberation?

A FULL PARDON
FOR MANKIND

YOU ARE ALL SONS OF GOD THROUGH FAITH IN CHRIST JESUS, FOR ALL OF YOU WHO WERE BAPTIZED INTO CHRIST HAVE CLOTHED YOURSELVES WITH CHRIST.... IF YOU BELONG TO CHRIST, THEN YOU ARE ABRAHAM'S SEED, AND HEIRS ACCORDING TO THE PROMISE.

(GALATIANS 3:26-27,29)

❧ TODAY'S DEVOTION ❧

Through Christ, our sins are forgiven and we receive a full pardon from God. A pardon is a powerful and potentially dangerous thing because it is irreversible. Once a king or ruler has pardoned someone, that person is forever free and exonerated of the crime or offense for which they were previously under judgment. Unlike a parole, which is a probationary state that still carries restrictions for the parolee, a pardon cleans the slate completely. A pardon declares its recipient to be as innocent as if the offense never occurred. Once a person is pardoned, the government returns his or her passport, and from that moment forward that person is free to travel, work, engage in business, buy and sell, and enjoy all other citizen rights and privileges without limitation. A pardon justifies and reestablishes a person's righteousness in the eyes of the law.

That is what Jesus did for all of us on the cross. His death and shed blood bought our pardon and made us righteous in the eyes of God once more. Our Kingdom citizenship and rights were restored, and we were positioned once again as recipients and heirs of all God's promises.

(Quote From *Rediscovering the Kingdom*, Pages 91-92)

QUESTIONS

1. Compare the difference between a pardon and a parole in terms of your own life before and after Christ. Do you live like you are pardoned or paroled?

2. How has your pardon freed you to engage in business for the Kingdom of God? What is the mind-set that you can possess to do business, that a parolee cannot have?

3. How has your pardon freed you from being guilty of breaking God's laws? Does it exonerate you from future sin?

4. When Jesus shed His blood for your pardon, He made you righteous in the eyes of God. Does that mean God cannot see your sins? How does this work?

5. As a pardoned person, you are positioned to receive God's promises. What one or two promises are you ready to receive at this time in your life? Take time to pray that you would remain in the receiving position.

MEDITATION

*"The word **righteous** is a legal term, not
a religious term, and means 'to position oneself
rightly.' Jesus came to make us righteous again, to put
us back in right relationship with God so that we
are qualified to receive the promises of God.
Understanding this is critical to developing solid
Kingdom thinking. When we are in right relationship
with God, He can extend His Kingdom—His
rulership—into our lives, and rule the earth through us.
It is as we rule the earth in the power and presence
of God that the Kingdom of heaven impacts
our planet through our physical lives"*
(Rediscovering the Kingdom, Page 91).

*Why is righteousness imperative to your rulership?
Answer this question in light of your personal
righteousness and your current ability to rule.*

DAY 15

ENTER THE KING AND THE KINGDOM

MANY ARE THE PLANS IN A MAN'S HEART, BUT IT IS THE LORD'S PURPOSE THAT PREVAILS.

(PROVERBS 19:21)

TODAY'S DEVOTION

There has been much controversy and debate down through the years over the life, message, death, and resurrection of Jesus Christ, especially within the religious community. There are many views and opinions as to what His real mission was. Scholars have dissected, examined, reviewed, revised and written volumes on these subjects. Yet many are still confused as to what His mission, message, methods, and purpose were for coming to earth.

However, for us to discover the original purpose and mission of Jesus, it should be obvious that we must consider His own declarations concerning His purpose and assignment for coming into the world....(See Matthew 10:7; 12:28; 18:23; 24:14, etc.)....[From these] declarations...it is obvious that His intent was to declare, establish, and invite all men to enter the Kingdom of God.

This is in direct contrast with the focus on religious activity and religion's preoccupation with going to heaven. It seems as if the message and priority of Jesus was the occupation and reclamation of earth, rather than designing an escape hatch to heaven for mankind.

(Quote From *Rediscovering the Kingdom,* Pages 98-100)

QUESTIONS

1. Why do you think there is so much confusion as to the real mission of Jesus Christ? What is the source of the confusion?

2. Jesus' intent was to declare the Kingdom of God. What are some things Jesus declared about the Kingdom?

3. Jesus' mission was to establish the Kingdom of God. In what ways did He do this? Where was it established?

4. Jesus' purpose was to invite all men to enter the Kingdom of God. Specifically, whom did Jesus invite? Were there representatives from all strata of society? Who responded to His invitation?

5. If our purpose is earth and not heaven-bound, how do most Christians need to make a course correction? Do you need a course change?

MEDITATION

*"The greatest tragedy in life is not death:
It is life without a purpose. The most important
discovery in life is the discovery of purpose. Purpose
is defined as the original intent or motivation for
something. Purpose is also defined as the reason
or desired result for the initiation or an action of
production of a thing. Simply put, purpose is the
'why' of a thing. Without a clear understanding of
purpose, life becomes an experiment. Where purpose
is not known, abuse is inevitable. Without purpose, activity
has no meaning and time and energy are misused. Purpose
determines what is right. Purpose protects us from doing
something good at the expense of the right. Purpose is
the predetermined, established, intended result of a thing"*
(Rediscovering the Kingdom, Page 97).

*Do you know your purpose in this life?
Do you see your activities and time in light
of your purpose? Take time to meditate on your
purpose and how your daily life reflects that purpose.*

Heaven's Ambassadors on Earth

And I confer on you a kingdom, just as My Father conferred one on Me.   (Luke 22:29)

Every nation appoints ambassadors and envoys to represent its interests to other nations. The Kingdom of heaven is no different, as it is the prototype of kingdoms. God chose to communicate the message of His Kingdom throughout the earth: not through *religious* people, but through *personal represen-tatives*. God's chosen strategy for proclaiming His Kingdom was to employ *ambassadors*. An ambassador is a political appointee whose job is to represent and speak for his or her home government before the rulers of other countries. In the eyes of those rulers, the word of an ambassador *is* the word of the government that he or she represents. Good ambassadors never speak their personal opinions, but only the official policies of the government that appointed them.

In the same way, the people of God are His ambassadors on the earth. Scripture clearly teaches this. God chose Moses to deliver the Israelites from slavery in Egypt and then to represent Himself before them. Prophets represented God and spoke His messages of warning and judgment to a nation that had turned away from Him....As ambassadors of heaven, we represent our Father's Kingdom on earth. If we are to be effective, it is important that we understand what we are talking about.

(Quote From *Rediscovering the Kingdom*, Page 101)

QUESTIONS

1. Why do you think God chose to communicate His Kingdom through personal representatives and not religious people? Is this avenue of communication widely known on the earth today? Why does mankind look to religious people for the "way" to know God?

2. Do you think of ambassadors as a country's representatives in a political, economic, social, or personal realm? What are God's ambassadors to represent? In what realm(s)?

3. If good ambassadors never speak their personal opinions, how well do you score on speaking only the official policies of the Kingdom of heaven?

4. When God chose Moses to represent Him, did Moses possess certain qualifications in order to be selected? Do you need to possess certain qualifications to be selected as a spokesperson for God?

5. When God spoke through the prophets, did He use a formula when telling them what to say and how and when to say it? Is there a certain formula that God uses when He speaks to you or when He uses you? Why or why not?

MEDITATION

*"The message of the Kingdom of God is
the most important news ever delivered to the
human race. Jesus came to earth to announce the
arrival of this Kingdom and to establish it in
people's hearts through His death and resurrection.
As the Son of God, Jesus Christ was the exact
likeness of His Father and represented Him perfectly
on earth. To all those who believed in and followed Him,
Jesus restored their citizenship rights in the Kingdom
of heaven and imparted His Spirit, so that they could
represent Him and the government of heaven on earth.
This representation is known as government diplomacy"*
(*Rediscovering the Kingdom*, Page 100).

*How does our diplomacy work on
earth? Are you a diplomatic representative
of God in your daily life?*

DAY 17

CHARACTERISTICS OF AN AMBASSADOR

AGAIN JESUS SAID, "PEACE BE WITH YOU! AS THE FATHER HAS SENT ME, I AM SENDING YOU." AND WITH THAT HE BREATHED ON THEM AND SAID, "RECEIVE THE HOLY SPIRIT." (JOHN 20:21-22)

An ambassador is a unique political creature in all kingdoms and his disposition must be understood fully, in order to appreciate the power and distinction of this revered position. Here are some very paramount qualities of an ambassador:

- Appointed by the king, not voted into position;
- Appointed to represent the state or kingdom;
- Committed only to the state's interests;
- Embodies the nation-state or kingdom;
- Totally covered by the state;
- Is the responsibility of the state;
- Totally protected by his government;
- Never becomes a citizen of the state or kingdom to which he is assigned;
- Can only be recalled by the king or president;
- Has access to all his nation's wealth for assignment;
- Never speaks his personal position on any issue, only his nation's official position; and,
- His goal is to influence the territory for his kingdom government....

All of these...apply to each citizen of the Kingdom of heaven who has been appointed by the government of heaven to represent heaven on earth. This is why Jesus admonished us to not worry about anything concerning our lives, but to focus on the kingdom; then everything we need for life and fulfilling our kingdom assignment on earth will be provided by the government of heaven.

(Quote From *Rediscovering the Kingdom,* Pages 101-102)

QUESTIONS

1. You are appointed by your King. Because you are not voted into position, what freedom does that give you? What restrictions?

2. You are a representative of the Kingdom of God. How does this influence the way in which you interact with people around you?

3. As an ambassador, you are on Kingdom business, committed only to the state's interests. How does this fact influence your view of your earthly purpose? How does it reorder your priorities?

4. As God's ambassador, you have access to all of the Kingdom resources you need for your assignment. How does this influence the way in which you view your finances and material possessions?

5. When you represent God, you are to influence the earth for His Kingdom. How do you currently do this? What are your next steps of influence?

MEDITATION

*"We are…ambassadors of our heavenly
government, representing our government's mind,
will, purposes and intent to the earth, so that His
kingdom can come and His will be done on earth just
as it is in heaven. We are charged only to speak what
our government speaks, not our own personal
opinion or views. Therefore, whenever an ambassador
is asked to comment on any issue, he is obligated
to speak his government's position. He simply quotes
the constitutional (the Bible) position on all matters.…
Study your constitution to know and understand your
government's position on all issues pertaining to life"*
(Rediscovering the Kingdom, Page 104).

So do it!

CONTRASTING A KINGDOM WITH A DEMOCRACY

WHO IS THIS THAT DARKENS MY COUNSEL WITH WORDS WITHOUT KNOWLEDGE? BRACE YOURSELF LIKE A MAN; I WILL QUESTION YOU, AND YOU SHALL ANSWER ME. WHERE WERE YOU WHEN I LAID THE EARTH'S FOUNDATION? TELL ME, IF YOU UNDERSTAND. (JOB 38:2-4)

A kingdom and a democracy are two totally different worlds. That is why it is difficult for believers who were born in a democracy to live a strong Kingdom life. We want to debate the issues or interject our own thoughts and opinions. We try to reach consensus or compromise to keep everyone happy instead of simply recognizing that the King's Word is law. If God says that adultery is a sin, that is the word of the King, and His Word is the law. The matter is not open for discussion. We can debate God's words and decrees until we are blue in the face, but in the end all we will have to show for it are blue faces; His Word will still be the law. No matter what humanistic philosophy preaches from its pulpits in the schools and in our courts, God's law is absolute.

In a democracy, citizens can gather to protest government policies and form committees and groups to lobby the legislative bodies to change laws. That does not happen in a kingdom. God's Word is absolute in His Kingdom, because it is set down for all to see in the Bible, which is the "constitution" of the Kingdom of God.

(Quote From *Rediscovering the Kingdom,* Page 106)

QUESTIONS

1. Contrast a kingdom and a democracy using the following chart:

Kingdom Characteristics	Democracy Characteristics

2. Looking at your chart, give reasons why many Christians consider the Kingdom of God to be a democracy.

3. Refer to your chart and tell what must change in the mind-set of Christians who believe the Kingdom of God is a democracy. How can this change be made?

4. How do the absolutes in God's Kingdom redefine Christianity from merely a religious choice among many, to the only choice possible?

5. What are some of the foundational items in the "constitution" of the Kingdom of God?

MEDITATION

"If we claim to be living the Kingdom life,
we cannot constantly be forming our own little
groups to advance our own opinions or to challenge
the Word of the King. As law, His Word is non-negotiable
and immutable. We run into problems every time we try
to carry our democratic mentality over into Kingdom life"
(*Rediscovering the Kingdom*, Page 107).

How often do your opinions conflict with
what God wants to do? Does a democratic
mentality interfere with your life in God's Kingdom?

BALANCING LIFE, WHILE LIVING IN TWO KINGDOMS

THEN HE SAID TO THEM, "GIVE TO CAESAR WHAT IS CAESAR'S, AND TO GOD WHAT IS GOD'S."

(MATTHEW 22:21)

As believers we face the daily challenge of living in two kingdoms at once: the Kingdom of heaven, where our citizenship lies, and the kingdom of this world, where we currently reside. The fact that these two kingdoms are often in conflict adds to the challenge....

As a Kingdom man, Jesus recognized that all governmental systems have legitimate claims and demands of their citizens. He simply said that we should give each kingdom its due. Every earthly kingdom has its own tax system. Because the coin used for paying the tax to Rome bore Caesar's picture, it meant that Caesar claimed it as his own. He was the king, and he was simply calling for that which was his. Whatever bore Caesar's image belonged to Caesar.

In the same manner, whatever bears God's image belongs to God. As beings created in the image of God, *we* belong to God, and He can claim us in a way no earthly kingdom can. The human leaders of the nation where we live and work and hold our citizenship may make legitimate claims on our time, our money, and our labor, but they have no claim on our character. We bear a deeper image and answer to a higher claim because we belong to God.

(Quote From *Rediscovering the Kingdom*, Pages 114-115)

QUESTIONS

1. As believers who live in two kingdoms, what types of challenges do we face? What challenges do you personally experience?

2. Why do these kingdoms come into conflict? In what ways have you seen a conflict between the Kingdom of God and earth's political systems?

3. Where do the two kingdoms differ in terms of our culture? What have you faced because of this difference?

4. How do the two kingdoms collide within your daily life? On the job? In the home? In your community?

5. What are the "legitimate claims on our time, our money, and our labor" of our earthly citizenship? How do these claims dictate how we conduct our lives? How does our citizenship of heaven supercede but not interfere with these legitimate claims?

MEDITATION

*"You may work in an office, and perhaps
your boss comes to you asking you to do something
that you know is not right. It may be unethical or
even illegal. What should you do? If you are
committed to Kingdom principles, you should
respectfully but firmly remind your boss that although
he can make demands of your time and your labor
while you are on the job, he cannot make demands
on your character. He may own the paper, the pencils,
the paper clips, the computer, and even the company,
but he does not own you. Stand up for what is right
even if it puts your job at risk. Once you sell your
character and integrity for the sake of your job, then
your boss **will** own you. Remember that you have
a deeper image on you and answer to a higher
authority because you belong to another Kingdom"*

(*Rediscovering the Kingdom*, Page 116).

*Have you ever had to face a situation such as
is described here? Are you able to answer
to your higher authority when necessary?*

THE ASSIGNMENT OF JESUS: RESTORE THE KINGDOM

THE SPIRIT OF THE LORD IS ON ME, BECAUSE HE HAS ANOINTED ME TO PREACH GOOD NEWS TO THE POOR. HE HAS SENT ME TO PROCLAIM FREEDOM FOR THE PRISONERS AND RECOVERY OF SIGHT FOR THE BLIND, TO RELEASE THE OPPRESSED, TO PROCLAIM THE YEAR OF THE LORD'S FAVOR. (LUKE 4:18-19)

God's purpose for us is the same as it has always been—to exercise dominion and authority over the earthly realm under His sovereign kingship. That has never changed. What *has* changed is our position. Adam and Eve's abdication of their rightful place of authority allowed satan, an unemployed cherub, to usurp the throne God intended for us to occupy....

Fortunately for us God did not simply write us off, wipe us out, and start all over. His eternal purpose will never be thwarted; His perfect will shall come to pass. From the very beginning, God had a plan that would resolve our defection: *"But when the time had fully come, God sent His Son, born of a woman, born under law, to redeem those under law, that we might receive the full rights of sons"* (Gal. 4:4-5). God's purpose was to restore us to our full status as His sons and daughters and bring us back into His Kingdom. He sent Jesus as the Way. Faith in Jesus Christ as the Son of God and in His death for our sins and resurrection for our life is the doorway through which we enter the Kingdom of God.

(Quote From *Rediscovering the Kingdom,* Page 119)

QUESTIONS

1. How has our position changed from what God originally intended? What kind of authority did we give to satan? How has this changed the way mankind operates in the world?

2. Explain Galatians 4:4-5 as you would to an unbeliever. How does this verse put the gospel in a nutshell?

3. Why did God send Jesus as "the Way" we would return to Him? Why couldn't mankind fulfill the obligation through the law?

4. What does the "full status as sons and daughters" entail? What responsibilities are included in that status? What benefits and blessings?

5. Luke 4:18-19 is a fulfillment of the Old Testament passage, Isaiah 61:1-2. How are we to fulfill this New Testament proclamation? How does the Kingdom of God multiply when we perform these activities?

MEDITATION

*"Everywhere He went, Jesus preached the
Kingdom. That was His assignment. Jesus' primary
message was not the born-again message that dominates
gospel preaching. In His entire recorded ministry,
Jesus spoke only once about being born again, and
that was in the middle of the night to a Pharisee
named Nicodemus who had come to Jesus privately.
Being born again is the way into the Kingdom—
it is the necessary first step. But the
gospel of the Kingdom involves much more"*
(Rediscovering the Kingdom, Page 122).

*What is your primary message as an
ambassador for the Kingdom? What more
is involved in the gospel of the Kingdom?
How well do you share the "more" with others?*

RESTORING OUR PLACE IN GOD'S PLAN

IF WE CLAIM TO HAVE FELLOWSHIP WITH HIM YET WALK IN THE DARKNESS, WE LIE AND DO NOT LIVE BY THE TRUTH.   (1 JOHN 1:6)

W hy is preaching the gospel of the Kingdom of God so important? Why did Jesus focus so singlemindedly on that message? It all has to do with God's unchangeable purpose. From the beginning, God's intent has been to extend His heavenly Kingdom onto the earth through mankind. That remains His intent, despite the fall of man. At first, Adam and Eve were completely fulfilled, fellowshipping with God and exercising their dominion authority as He intended. However, their sin and disobedience caused them to forfeit their authority. They lost the Kingdom.

The gospel of the Kingdom reveals how God is restoring us to our place, how He is taking us back from where we came. This is an important point to understand. Many of us assume or have been taught that the gospel means that God is preparing to take us to heaven as our home. That is not true restoration, because we did not come from heaven. Restoration means to put back in the original place or condition. Since we fell not from heaven but from our dominion authority on earth, being restored means putting us back in our place of earthly dominion.

(Quote From *Rediscovering the Kingdom,* Page 123)

QUESTIONS

1. First John 1:6 is not describing unbelievers; it is referring to those who are Christians. Explain what this verse means in light of its target audience.

2. Why is fellowship with Jesus while we are on earth so very important? How does this fellowship change how we see? (darkness or light) How does it affect how we live? (truth)

3. What is the purpose for Christians to live out their years on earth, if our message is only to prepare us for heaven? In what manner are our years of life on earth supposed to be lived?

4. How does the restoration of our dominion authority on earth happen? What causes this? What are the processes to achieve restoration?

5. Is it truly possible to be fully restored to our dominion authority while we live on earth? Why or why not? How much dominion do you take in your daily life?

MEDITATION

"One of God's biggest challenges in getting
His message of the Kingdom to the world is
the fact that we who are His representatives on earth
are so slow to understand the message. Dreams
of golden streets and heavenly bliss have blinded us
to our responsibilities on earth. We like to talk
about heaven because, for us, it represents for us
our highest goal and because it helps us get
our minds off of our problems here in the earth
realm. When we're busy singing 'I'll fly away,
O glory,' and 'When we all get to heaven, what
a day of rejoicing that will be,' it is easy to
forget—for a little while—our car trouble, our overdue
bills, the latest rent increase, or the job we just lost"
(*Rediscovering the Kingdom*, Page 124).

Are you challenged in the way described
here? What can be done to help Christians
understand this message?

DAY 22

THE POWER OF AN AMBASSADOR

For you are all sons of the light and sons of the day. We do not belong to the night or to the darkness. (1 Thessalonians 5:5)

Today's Devotion

Dominion authority is best illustrated in the function of ambassadors and embassies. Ambassadors are diplomats who carry out diplomacy for the government they represent. As Christ's ambassadors, we represent the Kingdom government of God. We are diplomats of His Kingdom in this world. Learning to see ourselves as ambassadors will change the way we think and live.

Whenever two nations establish formal diplomatic relations with each other, they open embassies in each other's capital city. The land on which each embassy is located is regarded as the sovereign territory of the nation whose embassy is located there. That sovereignty is recognized and respected by the government of the host nation as well as all other nations....For example, the United States' embassy in Nassau is American soil just as much as Miami, Washington, or New York. Even though it is located geographically on Bahamian soil, within its grounds the government of the Commonwealth of the Bahamas has no jurisdiction or authority....All the authority, rights, and powers of the nation represented by that government are in effect on that property. In the same way, we are ambassadors of Christ and of the Kingdom of God. Our home, office, church, and, indeed, anywhere our influence extends become an "embassy" of heaven.

(Quote From *Rediscovering the Kingdom*, Page 126)

1. As a diplomat of the Kingdom of God, how are you a part of the light and not the darkness? (See 1 Thessalonians 5:5.)

2. In what ways will "learning to see ourselves as ambassadors" change the way we live and think?

3. Where is the Kingdom of God's embassy on earth? Does it have more than one location?

4. What kind of protection does the Embassy of God's Kingdom afford you? Knowing this, is there any room for fear?

5. As an ambassador for the Kingdom of God, what kinds of influence are available to you? Do you exercise these kinds of influence regularly?

MEDITATION

*"Whenever we are in the presence of an
ambassador, we are in the presence of the
government he or she represents. The words
of the U.S. ambassador are the words of the
United States government. Diplomatically speaking,
they are one and the same. When we meet an
ambassador, we are meeting more than just
a person; we are meeting a nation"*
(*Rediscovering the Kingdom*, Page 127).

*What nation do people meet when
they meet with you? Are your words
reflective of the government of heaven?*

DAY 23

CITIZENS OF
A NEW ORDER

FROM THE DAYS OF JOHN THE BAPTIST UNTIL NOW, THE KINGDOM OF HEAVEN HAS BEEN FORCEFULLY ADVANCING, AND FORCEFUL MEN LAY HOLD OF IT.

(MATTHEW 11:12)

J esus was baptized by John in the Jordan River and was "full of the Holy Spirit."...Jesus was filled with the Holy Spirit without measure....He was the vanguard of a new order, the *first* of a new generation of people who would be filled with the Holy Spirit.

Jesus came to reconnect us to His Father and His glorious Kingdom. The connecting link is the Holy Spirit....Calvary then becomes the gateway into this majestic Kingdom. The essence of the gospel is that we can get back our spiritual connection to our Father. There is now a power available to us so that we can fulfill our role in the advancement of the Kingdom into the earth regions. This power is made available to us through an invasion of the Holy Spirit into our lives. Jesus opens up the door for that invasion to happen.

Jesus promised that He would give us the Kingdom and the power to walk in that Kingdom....Jesus' death on the cross was really a means to an end. Calvary became a cleansing fountain. Anyone who took the plunge into this fountain would become clean from the filth of living in this world. This cleansing would prepare them for receiving the power of the Holy Spirit.

(Quote From *Rediscovering the Kingdom,* Pages 131-132)

QUESTIONS

1. How was the way Jesus was filled with the Holy Spirit different from that of the Old Testament prophets? How was Jesus "filled with the Holy Spirit without measure"?

2. How did Jesus reconnect us to His Father? Does this reconnection happen when we die, or is the reconnection also for our earthly sojourn?

3. How does the Holy Spirit play an important role in reconnecting us to God's glorious Kingdom? What purpose does this reconnection play in our lives?

4. When the Holy Spirit invades our lives, how is power made available to us? What kind of power? To do what?

5. How is Calvary related to receiving the Holy Spirit? Why do we need to be cleansed before the Holy Spirit fills us?

MEDITATION

"Ever since the days of John, an invasion
has been under way. A military takeover is
in progress, which no one knows about except
those who have been captured. Have you been
taken over? I have been taken over—by the Kingdom
of heaven. It has taken over my heart, mind, soul, body,
and my entire future. It has taken over my attitude and
made me a dangerous man—to the kingdom of darkness"
(Rediscovering the Kingdom, Page 133).

Have you been taken over? Are you a
dangerous person to the kingdom of darkness?

THE GOOD NEWS OF THE KINGDOM

THEN THE KING WILL SAY TO THOSE ON HIS RIGHT, "COME, YOU WHO ARE BLESSED BY MY FATHER; TAKE YOUR INHERITANCE, THE KINGDOM PREPARED FOR YOU SINCE THE CREATION OF THE WORLD. FOR I WAS HUNGRY AND YOU GAVE ME SOMETHING TO EAT, I WAS THIRSTY AND YOU GAVE ME SOMETHING TO DRINK, I WAS A STRANGER AND YOU INVITED ME IN, I NEEDED CLOTHES AND YOU CLOTHED ME, I WAS SICK AND YOU LOOKED AFTER ME, I WAS IN PRISON AND YOU CAME TO VISIT ME."

(MATTHEW 25:34-36)

Acritical part of our introduction to the powerful truths of the Kingdom is about our inheritance as children of God....

Jesus is the King, but He is not our inheritance. Our inheritance is "the Kingdom prepared for [us] since the creation of the world." The gift that the King gives us is a Kingdom. We *inherit* the Kingdom, but Jesus *rules* the Kingdom....

As our inheritance, the Kingdom belongs to us by legal right. Adam and Eve lost the "papers" in the Garden and forfeited the Kingdom benefits, for themselves and their future generations. Jesus came to remove satan from his illegal occupation of the throne and make it possible for us to reclaim our inheritance. He is, in a sense, the executor of our estate. Even though our inheritance has been waiting for us since the creation of the world, we must go through Jesus to receive it....

In the spiritual realm, Christ is the mediator between God and man. He stands between the Kingdom and us. He mediates between our inheritance and us. We cannot receive the full benefits of our inheritance unless we go through Him. Just as [a trust fund might have been] ours as a child, even before we knew about it, even so is the Kingdom of God our inheritance from the foundation of the world.

(Quote From *Rediscovering the Kingdom,* Pages 140-142)

QUESTIONS

1. How does receiving our inheritance, provide proof that we are God's children?

2. "We *inherit* the Kingdom, but Jesus *rules* the Kingdom." What does this mean to you?

3. What throne has satan illegally occupied? Did Jesus remove him, or is he still ruling? What does his occupation have to do with whether we receive our inheritance or not?

4. Why must we go through Jesus to receive our inheritance? How does this separate Christianity from religions of this world?

5. Knowing your inheritance has been waiting for you since the foundation of the world, how do you feel about your importance in your Father's eyes?

MEDITATION

"Jesus says to us, 'There is a great
inheritance waiting for you, a Kingdom that
is yours, even though you knew nothing about it.
I am here to reveal it to you and help you claim it.
I am the Mediator. I am the Door. Come to Me,
trust in Me, and enter into the Kingdom prepared
for you.' When we take Jesus at His word, when
we trust Him as the one who can cleanse us of our
sin, when we give Him control and acknowledge Him
as Lord of our lives, we meet all the 'qualifications'
necessary to receive our Kingdom inheritance"
(*Rediscovering the Kingdom*, Page 142).

Do you take Jesus at His word? Do you trust
Him to cleanse you from sin? Do you give Him
control and acknowledge Him as Lord of your
life? Are you qualified to receive your inheritance?

DAY 25

LIFE INSIDE THE DOOR OF THE KINGDOM

I AM THE GATE; WHOEVER ENTERS THROUGH ME WILL BE SAVED. HE WILL COME IN AND GO OUT, AND FIND PASTURE. (JOHN 10:9)

"Life...to the max"—that's what our Kingdom inheritance is all about, and it *begins* with Jesus. But it does not end at the door. Remember that life is a journey and that life in the Kingdom will require that you move beyond your original experiences with God and mature and grow as a true son of the Kingdom.

Claiming our inheritance is not about joining a particular church or denomination. It has nothing to do with being "religious." It has *everything* to do with understanding that we are citizens of a Kingdom established and ruled by God, which will endure forever. As Kingdom citizens, we have legal rights to the government. The reason so many of us receive so little from God is because we do not recognize ourselves as citizens of His Kingdom, do not understand our rights as citizens, and therefore lack the confidence or boldness to *ask*. Kingdom citizenship is a spiritual reality, but it is also a *mentality*. As believers, we already have the Spirit of God, but we need to learn the *mind* and the *heart* of God. We need training in thinking and living as God's children.

(Quote From *Rediscovering the Kingdom*, Pages 143-144)

QUESTIONS

1. The pasture that Jesus brings us to is our inheritance. Describe that pasture in your own words.

2. Once inside the door, did you find it difficult to move beyond and experience new things in God? Why or why not?

3. How is our inheritance related to us growing and maturing as children of the Kingdom?

4. What are the legal rights you have claimed from the government of God's Kingdom? What do you still need to claim?

5. How does your mentality need to change so that you can receive all of your inheritance? What might your training look like in order to learn the mind and heart of God?

MEDITATION

*"Many believers get so completely fixated on Jesus as Savior and being 'born again' that as soon as they are inside the Kingdom, they camp out on the doorstep and never go any farther. Jesus is the **doorway** to the Kingdom; but, believe me, there are more riches that await inside"*

(*Rediscovering the Kingdom*, Page 143).

Do you know people who camp out on the doorstep of the Kingdom? Have you gone further? What riches have you discovered inside the door?

THE KINGDOM IS PREACHED IN WORD AND DEMONSTRATED IN POWER

THEREFORE GO AND MAKE DISCIPLES OF ALL NATIONS, BAPTIZING THEM IN THE NAME OF THE FATHER AND OF THE SON AND OF THE HOLY SPIRIT, AND TEACHING THEM TO OBEY EVERYTHING I HAVE COMMANDED YOU. AND SURELY I AM WITH YOU ALWAYS, TO THE VERY END OF THE AGE. (MATTHEW 28:19-20)

The nature of Jesus' proclamation was not just in the words He spoke. It was demonstrated in the power emanating from His life. The power of the Kingdom was demonstrated through Jesus by the miracles, signs, and wonders He performed. Crowds of people were drawn closer to the Kingdom by the words and actions of Jesus. The ones that "got the message" eventually became His followers and were introduced into fuller knowledge of who Jesus was and of how to enter the Kingdom through faith in Him....

It is really quite unfair to tell the world about Jesus Christ and the door that has been open to them without telling them about life on the other side of the door. It won't make sense....When we tell them of a domain where there is life, hope, peace, joy, and the power to rise above daily problems and difficulties *right now*, and live successfully and victoriously *right now*, they will say, "Hey, I can relate to that! I can understand that." As the church we must complete the message of Christ by focusing on the Kingdom of God, which was the heart of the words of Jesus.

(Quote From *Rediscovering the Kingdom,* Page 149)

QUESTIONS

1. Jesus proclaimed many principles of the Kingdom. Name three points that you feel are very foundational to all the words He spoke. How have these words of Jesus affected your life?

2. Jesus demonstrated the power of the Kingdom. Name three specific activities that exemplify the range of wonders He performed. How have the knowledge of these wonders affected your walk in the Kingdom?

3. How much of the job of "making disciples" has to do with the combination of *words* and *power*? Which of these two—words or power—seems to be the one most of us use? Why? How can we maintain a balance between the two?

4. Describe life on the "other side of the door" as you would to an unbeliever. Is everything rosy and bright in the earthly kingdom? What characterizes the domain that is above the earthly challenges we experience?

5. What does "living victoriously" mean? What is life in the Kingdom of God like? What benefits have you experienced that might give testimony to others?

MEDITATION

*"Life is hard and full of suffering and
pain. We live in a world of great anxiety. Terrorism,
economic collapse, political confusion, unemployment,
divorce, despair—people need good news. The
Kingdom of God is that good news. It is the lost
message of Jesus that needs to be resurrected in our times"*
(*Rediscovering the Kingdom,* Page 149).

*Who do you know that is currently experiencing
life's suffering and pain? Make a plan to resurrect
the lost message of Jesus to them in Word and power.*

EXPERIENCING HEAVEN ON EARTH

AFTER JOHN WAS PUT IN PRISON, JESUS WENT INTO GALILEE, PROCLAIMING THE GOOD NEWS OF GOD. "THE TIME HAS COME," HE SAID. "THE KINGDOM OF GOD IS NEAR. REPENT AND BELIEVE THE GOOD NEWS!"

(MARK 1:14–15)

The good news that John and Jesus preached—and that the early Church preached—was the good news of the *Kingdom* of heaven. So much of the time today we get the message wrong by preaching the good news of *heaven*. The two are not the same. We tell people to put their faith in Jesus for salvation and then we focus on heaven as our goal and destination. Jesus never preached heaven. His disciples never preached heaven, and neither should we. There may be a lot of appeal to the idea of going to heaven in the "sweet by-and-by," but people struggling with daily life on earth need a message to help them in the "sour now and now." People need to hear the good news of the Kingdom of heaven—the rule of God has come to earth and all can experience the reality of that world....

The comfort of heaven helps to keep us and sustain us through dark hours, but it is not and should never be the focus of the gospel we preach. Scripture promises us not that Jesus would rescue us from a world on the brink of overcoming us, but that in Him we would overcome the world.

(Quote From *Rediscovering the Kingdom,* Pages 155-156)

QUESTIONS

1. Explain the difference between heaven and the Kingdom. What does the difference mean to you as a believer?

2. What message does the Kingdom of God bring to people who are struggling with daily life? How has the message helped you?

3. What does "the rule of God has come to earth" mean to you? What does it mean to unbelievers? To believers?

4. What place does the knowledge of heaven "in the sweet by-and-by" have in our story of the Kingdom? What help has this knowledge had for you?

5. How are we to overcome the world? What does it take for us to become part of the overcoming army?

MEDITATION

"Overcoming the world…means that when
we live and think and act like Kingdom citizens,
we can experience success, victory, and fruitfulness,
not in the 'sweet by-and-by,' but today, this week.
It means that we can overcome **right now**. *We don't*
have to be or remain victims of our circumstances.
We can avail ourselves of our Kingdom citizenship
and all its blessings, rights, and benefits to help us
rise above our circumstances, either to change them,
or to prosper and move forward in spite of them.
Kingdom living does not sit back meekly in
submission and defeat before the onslaught of the
world. Kingdom living moves forward with
confidence, advancing forcefully in the wisdom,
H.G.+
resurrection
power, and boldness that are ours as children of God"
(Rediscovering the Kingdom, Page 156).

Have you felt that you were a victim
of circumstances at any time in your
life? Why is this wrong thinking?

A KINGDOM OF SERVANT KINGS

42 Generation

BUT YOU ARE A CHOSEN PEOPLE, A ROYAL PRIESTHOOD, A HOLY NATION, A PEOPLE BELONGING TO GOD, THAT YOU MAY DECLARE THE PRAISES OF HIM WHO CALLED YOU OUT OF DARKNESS INTO HIS WONDERFUL LIGHT. ONCE YOU WERE NOT A PEOPLE, BUT NOW YOU ARE THE PEOPLE OF GOD; ONCE YOU HAD NOT RECEIVED MERCY, BUT NOW YOU HAVE RECEIVED MERCY. (1 PETER 2:9-10)

The kingdom of God is the only kingdom in which every citizen is designated a king. Their rulership is not over people, but in a specific area of gifting. This is why Jesus is referred to as the King of kings and Lord of lords. We are kings who serve the world with our God-given gift. We serve our way into leadership. This is what Jesus meant when He said, "the greatest among you shall be your servant." The kingdom functions on the basis of servant leadership.

Once we have entered the door, there is nothing that is more vital to our spiritual growth than to understand the nature of the Kingdom of which we are now citizens. Our hearts should reflect Christ's heart, and our minds, His mind. The Kingdom represents the heart of the entire work of God. Everything God says and does relates to His Kingdom. That is why it is so important that we understand its nature. If we are to be faithful children of the King and ready to rule the dominion He has given us, we must know His heart and how to rule in His name.

(Quote From *Rediscovering the Kingdom*, Page 161)

QUESTIONS

1. What does "rulership [in the Kingdom] is not over people, but in a specific area of gifting" mean to you? Have you ever felt like a ruler in your area of gifting? What is the area(s) where you rule?

2. If Jesus is King of kings, does this mean He is King over all other earthly political monarchs, or over us, His servant-kings? Explain your answer.

3. How does a Christian serve his way into leadership? What qualities does servanthood bring to leadership? What qualities does leadership bring to servanthood?

4. How do your God-given gifts reflect the Kingdom of God? How do they show the heart of God?

5. How can you improve the rulership you have through your gifts? Are there ways you can reflect more of the Kingdom?

MEDITATION

*"Our culture is disintegrating all around us.
People are living in despair. All we have to do
is read a newspaper or listen to a news broadcast
any day of the week to realize that daily life in the
world we live in is full of uncertainty and instability....
Because the kingdom of this world is temporary and
will one day pass away, it has nothing of enduring
quality in which we can trust with any confidence"*

(Rediscovering the Kingdom, Page 161).

*What good news do we have for such a world?
Are you sharing the good news with anyone
who is overwhelmed with the world situation?*

DAY 29

A DISTURBANCE IN THE FORCE

AND I WILL ASK THE FATHER, AND HE WILL GIVE YOU ANOTHER COUNSELOR TO BE WITH YOU FOREVER— THE SPIRIT OF TRUTH. THE WORLD CANNOT ACCEPT HIM, BECAUSE IT NEITHER SEES HIM NOR KNOWS HIM. BUT YOU KNOW HIM, FOR HE LIVES WITH YOU AND WILL BE IN YOU. (JOHN 14:16–17)

JESUS

❧ TODAY'S DEVOTION ❧

The key to man's being able to manifest the Kingdom of God here on earth is the presence of the Holy Spirit. Man cannot know God's will except through the Holy Spirit living within him, and the Holy Spirit can live only in a holy vessel. Adam and Eve...were filled with the Holy Spirit and enjoyed intimate fellowship with God. When they were seduced and deceived by satan's temptation and disobeyed God, that line of communication was broken, creating a disturbance in the force of the universe....They became unholy vessels, and the Holy Spirit departed, cutting off their connection with the heavenly realm....

In Jesus Christ, the Holy Spirit returned to earth to dwell in full force in a human being for the first time since leaving Adam and Eve....The man Jesus was flesh, but the Christ within was full of the Spirit. He was Jesus Christ, the God-man, God in the flesh. In Him the fullness of God dwelled in bodily form (see Col. 2:9). That fullness was the Holy Spirit, who was now abiding and dwelling in human flesh for the first time since Eden. Jesus modeled for all mankind the spiritual potential that could belong to them if they were empowered by the Spirit of God.

(Quote From *Rediscovering the Kingdom*, Pages 166-167)

Handwritten annotations:

in cool even

ZOE

Pentcost

The Second ADAM = 777 = Perfect = He died! went to hell

Spirit Soul Body

then on 3rd. Day He arose

new Beginnings

The LAST ADAM = 888 = He LIVES Forever in Heaven above all!

Spirit Soul Body

QUESTIONS

1. Explain why the Holy Spirit is so key to the Kingdom of God on earth.

2. How does a lack of holiness prevent the Holy Spirit from dwelling within us? Can anyone really be holy? Why or why not?

3. How did Jesus bring the ability to communicate with God back to us?

4. How does the Holy Spirit dwell in us? What is His "fullness"?

5. What spiritual potential do you have? How will you see this potential realized?

MEDITATION

*"When Jesus, full of the Holy Spirit, began
His public ministry, His message was the
simple announcement, **'Repent, for the kingdom
of heaven is near'** (Mt. 4:17)....Jesus was
saying, 'Repent, change your mind because your
thoughts are corrupt.' Why are they corrupt? Because
of sin. Why should we change our minds? Because
the Kingdom of heaven is near....It is here now, and
we need to adjust our thinking to that **new** reality"*

(Rediscovering the Kingdom, Pages 167–168).

*In what ways do you need to adjust
your thinking to the new reality?*

TRAINING TO BECOME ROYALTY IN THE HEAVENLY KINGDOM

B UT WHEN HE, THE SPIRIT OF TRUTH, COMES, HE WILL GUIDE YOU INTO ALL TRUTH. HE WILL NOT SPEAK ON HIS OWN; HE WILL SPEAK ONLY WHAT HE HEARS, AND HE WILL TELL YOU WHAT IS YET TO COME. (JOHN 16:13)

[handwritten: JESUS]

[handwritten: the Family of]

[handwritten: We no. the 42 generation of Christ one's = abraham Sarah]

As children of God, we are part of the royal family of the Kingdom of heaven. Like any other member of royalty, we don't just step into the role without any preparation; we must be trained. Proper and careful training is essential for rulers in the making....

/ We must learn how to think and act like the royal children of the heavenly King. We have spent so long in the condition and mentality of slaves in the kingdom of darkness that we automatically think and act like slaves. If we are to exercise our full status and potential in the earthly realm as ambassadors of our Father, we must be retrained in the behavior and mindset of the Kingdom. In this task, the Holy Spirit is our tutor....

[handwritten: like Egypt 666]

[handwritten: GOD]

[handwritten: 888]

When we first become believers, we receive our new spiritual birth from Jesus Christ, who then "turns us over," in a manner of speaking, to someone else—the Holy Spirit—for our training and upbringing as children of the King....In His earthly incarnation, Jesus could not be continuously and physically present with all His followers, so He promised to send His Spirit who would abide with us forever and teach us how to think and act like the royalty we are.

[handwritten: also angels]

(Quote From *Rediscovering the Kingdom,* Pages 172-174)

JESUS

QUESTIONS

1. What are the training components that will prepare us for our role as royalty? What components have you learned thus far?

2. What is the difference between a slave mentality and a son mentality? How must our thought patterns change so that we can acquire the right mentality?

3. What are the types of behavior that reflect Kingdom royalty? How "natural" does this behavior come to you?

4. Research Scriptures that tell how the Holy Spirit trains and guides us as believers. Choose one of these to memorize to remind you of your progressive training.

5. When does our training end? How can we remain teachable so that the Holy Spirit can continue to train us?

We "Never" Ending Training ~ to H.S.
Humble Ourself   Listen to H.S.
Like Little children + obey His Voice'

MEDITATION

*"One of the things the Holy Spirit teaches
us is how to stand in authority as true sons and
daughters of God no matter what troubles or difficulties
come into our lives. As royal children of our heavenly
Father, we can take charge of our circumstances, rather
than being a slave to them. We can live daily in power
and victory, rather than in weakness and defeat. All
it takes is training, and the Holy Spirit is our Teacher"*
(Rediscovering the Kingdom, Page 175).

*What characterizes your life...slavery to troubles
and difficulties, or living in power and victory over
those troubles? In what ways do you need to improve?*

YOUR PLACE
IN THE KINGDOM

As you come to Him, the living Stone—rejected by men but chosen by God and precious to Him—you also, like living stones, are being built into a spiritual house to be a holy priesthood, offering spiritual sacrifices acceptable to God through Jesus Christ. (1 Peter 2:4-5)

Each of us who turn to Christ become a "stone" in the magnificent spiritual "palace" of the Kingdom of God on earth, called and equipped as kings and priests to represent that Kingdom before the rest of the world....

Throughout human history, the religious society has generally separated priest and king into separate offices and functions, but God did not design them that way in the beginning. When God created us, He intended for us to be His representative rulers—His ambassadors—over the rest of the created order. We were to be priests/kings in the earth: as priests, representing God's nature and character, and as kings, His Kingdom government.

Through Christ we are a "holy priesthood," a "chosen people," a "royal priesthood," and a "holy nation." As such, we have been restored to our priestly function of representing and reflecting God's nature and character before the world. We are also the "people of God," not a nation of subjects, but of sons and daughters. If God is a King, then we, His people, are also of the royal line. Therefore, we have also been restored to our kingly function of representing the government of God on the earth.

(Quote From *Rediscovering the Kingdom,* Page 178)

QUESTIONS

1. What does it mean to you to be a stone in the spiritual palace of the Kingdom of God? What is a "living stone"?

2. What is your job description as a king in the Kingdom of God?

3. What is your job description as a priest in the Kingdom of God?

4. How do the job descriptions of king and priest combine to fulfill the mission of the Kingdom of God?

5. Among these four—"holy priesthood," a "chosen people," a "royal priesthood," and a "holy nation"—which do you find easiest to identify with and why?

MEDITATION

"God is not interested in having subjects
in His Kingdom. He wants only children, royal
heirs to the treasures of His domain. Our mission
as ambassadors of the Kingdom of God is to bring
those who are enslaved in the kingdom of darkness
to Christ, the door, so that He can set them free to
enter into their full citizenship in God's Kingdom of light"
(*Rediscovering the Kingdom,* Page 178).

Pray for the Lord to reveal the next
person who you should introduce to his or her
awaiting citizenship in the Kingdom of God.

DAY 32

KINGS, PROPHETS, AND THE KINGDOM

"AND YOU SHALL BE TO ME A KINGDOM OF PRIESTS AND A HOLY NATION." THESE ARE THE WORDS THAT YOU SHALL SPEAK TO THE SONS OF ISRAEL.

(EXODUS 19:6 NAS)

Normally, when we talk about the Kingdom of God, we think only of what Jesus said about the subject as recorded in the four Gospels. Although it is certainly true that in His life and words Jesus revealed the Kingdom more fully than ever before, they were simply the culmination of all that God had been working toward from the beginning, as was His life in general. Everything God says and does relates to His Kingdom. The entire Bible deals with the Kingdom of God. From Genesis to Revelation, Scripture reveals God as the great and almighty King of heaven and earth resolutely at work on His plan of the ages....

Everything centers on the Kingdom of God. All the saints of the Old Testament recognized this fact.... The prophets knew it. Jesus knew it. All the apostles and other believers in the New Testament knew it. Everyone, it seems, understood the priority of the Kingdom; everyone except us, that is. In recent years the focus in much of the Body of Christ has shifted away from the Kingdom of God to other issues. The tragic result is that multitudes of believers today know little about the Kingdom, and even fewer understand their place and rights as its citizens.

(Quote From *Rediscovering the Kingdom,* Pages 181-182)

QUESTIONS

1. Look up four or five Old Testament Scriptures that deal with the Kingdom of God. What do they tell you about the Kingdom?

2. How did Jesus reveal the Kingdom even more fully than the Old Testament writers?

3. How did the writers of the Epistles reveal the Kingdom of God?

4. Based on what you know of the Church today, how has the focus shifted away from the Kingdom of God?

5. How would you suggest that we advertise the Kingdom of God to a greater degree?

MEDITATION

"Often, even in spite of all our sophistication, education, and technology, we of modern and 'enlightened' democratic societies are worse off than the people of Old Testament times when it comes to matters of understanding the Kingdom of God and how our world relates to it"
(*Rediscovering the Kingdom,* Page 182).

Explain the previous sentence in terms of what you have experienced. How are you "worse off" than the people in the Old Testament in understanding the Kingdom?

A Kingdom Made Not by Human Hands

N<small>O ONE IS LIKE</small> Y<small>OU</small>, O L<small>ORD</small>; Y<small>OU ARE GREAT, AND</small> Y<small>OUR NAME IS MIGHTY IN POWER</small>. W<small>HO SHOULD NOT REVERE</small> Y<small>OU</small>, O K<small>ING OF THE NATIONS</small>? T<small>HIS IS</small> Y<small>OUR DUE</small>. A<small>MONG ALL THE WISE MEN OF THE NATIONS AND IN ALL THEIR KINGDOMS, THERE IS NO ONE LIKE</small> Y<small>OU</small>.

(J<small>EREMIAH</small> 10:6-7)

To Jeremiah God was "King of the nations," "the true God...the living God, the eternal King" whom people of all the nations should revere and honor. As King, God sat rightfully as Judge of the earth, and under His wrath and anger the nations could not endure. What a powerful picture of God! Jeremiah knew God as a King who was truly sovereign over His entire domain, both spiritual and physical. The strongest and most fearsome of human kingdoms are nothing in comparison to the Kingdom of God....

What this means for us is that, even though satan and the forces of darkness are still around to harass us if we let them, their power and authority over us have been broken. They have already been judged. Their final destruction awaits the consummation of all things with the return of Christ, but it is as certain as though it had already happened. This is why we do not have to surrender to defeat or despair or helplessness in our daily lives. We can live in victory and walk in confidence because the power of our enemy has been broken. The Lord has given us authority over him. We are among those seated in judgment over him with the King.

(Quote From *Rediscovering the Kingdom,* Pages 186, 191)

QUESTIONS

1. Look at the picture Jeremiah paints of God. How does it make you feel to have the King of the nations as your Leader?

2. What does it mean to you to have the true God, the living God, and the eternal King as your Father? I can relate to him in an understandable way, and I must Respect Him for Who He IS = GOD! my yet PaPa also. I love + Fear him — GOD + my Holy Papa

3. Understanding God's sovereignty can bring peace to your heart. What issues does His sovereignty settle? as a Child Loves! Her Daddy yet fears his Spankings if I dis-obeyed him.

4. How does God's authority give us victory over defeat, despair, and helplessness?

The "Greater One lives in Me/US! Jesus is Our Head + We his Body alive.

5. Do you walk in confidence that you have authority over satan? Yes! Why or why not? What does it mean that you are among those, with the King, seated in judgment over satan?

Because Jesus "lives" BIG" in Me NOW! and told me too of I Believe Him. It is Satan is under Our Feet. I written As we are in Him, Christ Jesus Our LORD!

MEDITATION

*"David understood his role not only
as a king under God with civic obligations
to his people, but also as a priest before God
with spiritual responsibilities on behalf of his
people. He is an example to all of us of our
place in the Kingdom. Like David we are called
to rule as kings in this world as well as to fulfill
the priestly role of carrying out our spiritual
care of the people in the earthly regions"*
(*Rediscovering the Kingdom*, Page 184).

*Using David as an example, what is
your place in the Kingdom as a king and a priest?*

THE SAINTS GET THE KINGDOM

THEN THE SOVEREIGNTY, POWER AND GREATNESS OF THE KINGDOMS UNDER THE WHOLE HEAVEN WILL BE HANDED OVER TO THE SAINTS, THE PEOPLE OF THE MOST HIGH. HIS KINGDOM WILL BE AN EVERLASTING KINGDOM, AND ALL RULERS WILL WORSHIP AND OBEY HIM.

(DANIEL 7:27)

We did not come from heaven, nor were we created for heaven....What we lost at the fall was not heaven, but the Kingdom. Jesus died on the cross and rose from the dead not so much to take us to heaven as to bring us back into possession of the Kingdom we lost. When we receive it, we will possess it forever and ever....

Daniel 7:27 mentions three specific things that the children of God will receive when they come into the Kingdom:

- Sovereignty;

- Power; and,

- Greatness.

Sovereignty means absolute authority....God is the only *true* Sovereign because He is answerable to no one except Himself. All other sovereignty is delegated sovereignty, which implies a delegator who is greater. Within the scope of our delegated sovereignty, we have absolute authority....

When Jesus restored the Kingdom to us, He did not give us a pretty façade with nothing inside. Along with the Kingdom He gave us *power*: power to overcome, prosper, live in victory, be joyful, and to fulfill our potential.

Finally, with the Kingdom comes *greatness*....When we are restored to the Kingdom, we are restored to greatness, because we return to the place and environment for which we were created.

(Quote From *Rediscovering the Kingdom*, Pages 193-194)

QUESTIONS

1. Explain what you think the author means when he says, "Jesus died...not so much to take us to heaven as to bring us back into possession of the Kingdom we lost."

2. What does this mean to you: "Within the scope of our delegated sovereignty, we have absolute authority"?

3. Look at the three things Daniel 7:27 says we will receive when we come into the Kingdom. How will we receive the sovereignty? What purpose will our sovereignty serve the Kingdom?

4. How will we receive power when we come into the Kingdom? What will our power do to serve the Kingdom of God?

5. How will we become great as we come into the Kingdom? How will our greatness serve God's Kingdom?

MEDITATION

*"Jesus said that the key to true greatness
is humility and service....We were not created
to dominate each other, or to be dominated, but
to serve one another equally as kings and priests
in our Father's Kingdom. It is only when we
understand our place and role in the Kingdom that
we can fully appreciate the meaning of greatness"*
(*Rediscovering the Kingdom*, Page 194).

According to the definition here, how great are you?

THE PRIORITY OF THE KINGDOM

HE SAID TO THEM, "GO INTO ALL THE WORLD AND PREACH THE GOOD NEWS TO ALL CREATION."

(MARK 16:15)

How important is the Kingdom of God? It is so important that our lives depend on it, literally. All that we are, all that we see and hear, the air we breathe, the food we eat, the water we drink—this physical world of ours issued forth from the Kingdom of God by His hand at creation. The Kingdom of God is at the center of everything. God's every action and activity is motivated by His desire and passion to see His Kingdom established on the earth.

How important to the Body of Christ is the message of the Kingdom of God? Frankly, we have nothing else to preach or teach. The message of the Kingdom is good news, and the Church exists to proclaim it. If we are doing our job, everything we are about will be Kingdom-focused: every sermon we preach, every Bible study we teach, every ministry we perform, every activity we accomplish, and every worship service we celebrate.

The Kingdom of God must be our highest priority; Jesus gave us no other commission. When He said, "Go and make disciples of all nations," He was commanding us to proclaim the Kingdom of God to a world that knew it not.

(Quote From *Rediscovering the Kingdom*, Page 197)

QUESTIONS

1. Why do our lives depend on the Kingdom of God? Is it a life or death dependence?

2. How has the physical world issued forth from the Kingdom of God? Is it our "environmental protection agency?" How does this put to death the myth of Mother Nature?

3. "God's every action and activity is motivated by His desire and passion to see His Kingdom established on the earth." Explain this in terms of your own desires and passions.

4. If the message of the Kingdom of God is the only message we have to preach, why do so many get off on tangents, or major in minor issues? What kind of a distraction is this to the Body of Christ?

5. We are commanded to make disciples. It is not a request. Does this mean everyone has the gift of evangelism? Why or why not?

MEDITATION

*"Although the world is very familiar with
the regimes of men, it is essentially ignorant of
God's Kingdom. People of every nation need to know
that God's Kingdom has come to earth, and that faith
in Jesus Christ as Savior and Lord is the way in"*
(*Rediscovering the Kingdom*, Page 197).

*Do you know people who are essentially
ignorant of God's Kingdom? Are there
ways you might be able to educate them?*

DAY 36

FATHER IS ALWAYS WORKING

Jesus said to them, "My Father is always at his work to this very day, and I, too, am working...."

(John 5:17)

The Jewish religious leaders took Jesus to task for working on the Sabbath. Jesus' reply was that He simply was following the example of His Father: "My Father is always at His work...and I, too, am working." ...

The important point here is that Jesus, as the Son of His Father, was committed to working whenever His Father worked, and doing whatever His Father was doing. Since the Father was always working, Jesus was always working, whether or not it was the Sabbath. Besides, Jesus plainly said, "The Sabbath was made for man, not man for the Sabbath. So the Son of Man is Lord even of the Sabbath" (Mark 2:27-28). God never intended for us to be slaves, bound to a strict legalistic interpretation of the day of "rest," but to live as free people in doing what is right and good at all times. By word and by example, Jesus showed us that it is *always* right to do good, even on the Sabbath.

As children of our Father, we also should be working whenever He is working. Jesus, as our elder brother, has set the example for us. The good work of the Kingdom of God never takes a holiday, and neither should we.

(Quote From *Rediscovering the Kingdom*, Pages 202-203)

QUESTIONS

1. Jesus broke the religious "laws" about the Sabbath. Should we have the same freedom to break "laws" that the church has set for this day? Why or why not?

2. How did Jesus know what the Father was doing? How can we know? When does the Father sleep? Why do we need to sleep when the Father does not?

3. Explain the balance between observing the day of rest and always working, even on the Sabbath.

4. If we "live as free people" in regards to the Sabbath, does this open it up for multiple interpretations of what should and should not be done on the Sabbath?

5. Define what "doing good" is. If it is "always right" to do good...when do we get a day off?

MEDITATION

*"Even when we are on vacation, and at
other times when we are not at work at our jobs,
we should still be working for the Kingdom.
Too many times, when believers go on vacation
they also take a break from the Lord and His church;
they don't attend worship anywhere, they don't send
in their tithe, they don't study God's Word, and
they don't talk to anyone about the Lord and
His Kingdom. This is not right. The work
of the Kingdom never stops. Our Father is
always working, and we should be working also"*
(*Rediscovering the Kingdom*, Page 203).

*Do you think the fact that we are
24/7 workers for the Kingdom is too
stressful for human beings? Why or why not?*

PRIESTS WHO ARE ALSO KINGS

AND FROM JESUS CHRIST, WHO IS THE FAITHFUL WITNESS, THE FIRSTBORN FROM THE DEAD, AND THE RULER OF THE KINGS OF THE EARTH. TO HIM WHO LOVES US AND HAS FREED US FROM OUR SINS BY HIS BLOOD, AND HAS MADE US TO BE A KINGDOM AND PRIESTS TO SERVE HIS GOD AND FATHER—TO HIM BE GLORY AND POWER FOR EVER AND EVER! AMEN. (REVELATION 1:5-6)

God's original plan was for both king and priest to be the same person, but ever since the fall mankind has been trying to keep the two separate....*God has always wanted a priest with a crown*....Jesus is the example, the prototype of what God desires for all His children. He wants us to be like Jesus, kings and priests in the world: kings to faithfully represent His government and execute His authority on the earth. He wants us to be priests who will represent His love, grace, and mercy to a world of people stumbling in the darkness with no knowledge either of Him or of His Kingdom. This is the purpose that lies behind His call to each of us when we came to Christ....

We, the Church, the "called-out ones" of Jesus Christ, are "a chosen people, a royal priesthood, a holy nation" called of God to "declare" His praises to a dark world. A royal priesthood is another way of saying that each one of us is both a king and a priest. Our Lord has called and commissioned each of us as His ambassadors—His agents—in leading those still trapped in darkness into the "wonderful light" of His Kingdom.

(Quote From *Rediscovering the Kingdom,* Pages 209-211)

QUESTIONS

1. What effect did the fall have in keeping the roles of king and priest separate? Have you thought of these as one role before reading this book?

2. Why is a priest with a crown a more effective way to represent the Kingdom than having two different offices?

3. How can we execute God's authority on earth and at the same time represent His love, grace, and mercy? How can these be wrapped in the same package?

4. As a king and priest serving God (see Rev. 1:5-6), how are you performing your service? Is it easy or difficult for you? Are you mostly effective or ineffective?

5. The Lord has commissioned you for service—it is not optional or on a when-you-feel-like-it basis. What does your Kingdom responsibility do to change your perspective of your daily activities?

MEDITATION

"As followers of Christ, children of God,
and citizens of His realm, we have no priority
greater than proclaiming His Kingdom....Through
His Spirit He has called each of us back home
to our rightful place as royal citizens so that we
can exercise our rights and authority right now
and experience the victory of Kingdom living on
a daily basis. He has also invited us to join Him
in His work of reconciling the world to Himself"

(*Rediscovering the Kingdom,* Page 211).

Does the progression this paragraph describes
seem too good to be true? How can this become reality?

UNDERSTANDING THE KINGDOM CONCEPTS—PART A

THEY WILL MAKE WAR AGAINST THE LAMB, BUT THE LAMB WILL OVERCOME THEM BECAUSE HE IS LORD OF LORDS AND KING OF KINGS—AND WITH HIM WILL BE HIS CALLED, CHOSEN AND FAITHFUL FOLLOWERS.

(REVELATION 17:14)

TODAY'S DEVOTION

All true kingdoms contain the same characteristics and components. Here are concepts and principles of kingdoms that you should know and become familiar with. Study and apply them to the message of the Kingdom of God and heaven taught by the King Himself, Jesus Christ, in order to fully understand your purpose, potential, power, and position in life.

1. The Kingdom Principle of Kings: The king is the central component of a kingdom and embodies the essence of the kingdom.

I BELIEVE THIS PRINCIPLE MEANS: _____

TO APPLY THIS PRINCIPLE TO MY LIFE, I NEED TO: _____

_____

2. The Kingdom Lordship Principle: All true kings must have property or a domain over which they exercise rulership of dominion.

I BELIEVE THIS PRINCIPLE MEANS: _____

TO APPLY THIS PRINCIPLE TO MY LIFE, I NEED TO: _____

_____

3. The Kingdom Domain Principle: The domain of a king is the territory over which he exercises authority, control, and dominion.

I BELIEVE THIS PRINCIPLE MEANS: _____

TO APPLY THIS PRINCIPLE TO MY LIFE, I NEED TO: _____

_____

4. The Kingdom Constitution Principle: The constitution of the kingdom is the documented will, intent, desires, and purposes of the king for his citizens and kingdom.

I BELIEVE THIS PRINCIPLE MEANS: _____

TO APPLY THIS PRINCIPLE TO MY LIFE, I NEED TO: _____

_____

5. The Kingdom Law Principle: The law of the kingdom is the proclaimed word, decrees, and edicts of the king, and these laws determine the standards and precepts by which the kingdom is to be governed.

I BELIEVE THIS PRINCIPLE MEANS: _____

TO APPLY THIS PRINCIPLE TO MY LIFE, I NEED TO: _____

---

6. The Kingdom Keys Principle: The keys of the kingdom are the principles, precepts, laws, and systems by which the kingdom functions.

I BELIEVE THIS PRINCIPLE MEANS: _____

TO APPLY THIS PRINCIPLE TO MY LIFE, I NEED TO: _____

---

7. The Kingdom Citizenship Principle: Citizenship in a kingdom is not a right but a privilege, and it is at the pleasure of the king himself.

I BELIEVE THIS PRINCIPLE MEANS: _____

TO APPLY THIS PRINCIPLE TO MY LIFE, I NEED TO: _____

---

8. The Kingdom Royal Privilege Principle: Royal privileges of the kingdom are the benefits the king affords his citizens.

I BELIEVE THIS PRINCIPLE MEANS: _____

TO APPLY THIS PRINCIPLE TO MY LIFE, I NEED TO: _____

(Quote From *Rediscovering the Kingdom,* Pages 215-219)

MEDITATION

"I challenge you to embrace and accept
the invitation of the King, Jesus Christ, to come
and renew your citizenship in the Kingdom of heaven
by being born into the Kingdom of God through
the reception of the Holy Spirit of the King, by
accepting the provision of the redemptive work
of the King Himself. This is your opportunity, not
to join a religion or become a slave of rituals or
traditions that have no practical meaning, but rather
to migrate from the kingdom of darkness to the Kingdom of
light and renew your heavenly immigration status on earth"
(*Rediscovering the Kingdom*, Pages 226-227).

If you have accepted Christ as your Savior
but have not understood the ramifications of His
Kingdom once you have committed your life to Christ,
renew your commitment and begin a new journey to
put these principles into your mind, heart, and daily life.

UNDERSTANDING THE KINGDOM CONCEPTS—PART B

THEY ARE NOT OF THE WORLD, EVEN AS I AM NOT OF IT. (JOHN 17:16)

Here are more concepts and principles of kingdoms that you should know and become familiar with. Study and apply them to the message of the Kingdom of God and heaven taught by Jesus, in order to fully understand your purpose, potential, power, and position in life.

9. The Kingdom Code of Ethics Principle: This is the standard of conduct established by the king for the behavior and social relationships of his citizens.

I BELIEVE THIS PRINCIPLE MEANS: _____

TO APPLY THIS PRINCIPLE TO MY LIFE, I NEED TO:_____

_____

10. The Kingdom Commonwealth Principle: All kingdoms function on the principle of a commonwealth. Commonwealth is the king's commitment to see that all of his citizens have equal access to the wealth and resources of the kingdom.

I BELIEVE THIS PRINCIPLE MEANS: _____

TO APPLY THIS PRINCIPLE TO MY LIFE, I NEED TO:_____

_____

11. The Kingdom Culture Principle: This is the lifestyle and way of life for the citizens manifested in their language, dress, eating habits, values, morals, and sense of self-worth and self-concept.

I BELIEVE THIS PRINCIPLE MEANS: _____

TO APPLY THIS PRINCIPLE TO MY LIFE, I NEED TO:_____

_____

12. The Kingdom Economy Principle: All kingdoms operate on a system that secures and sustains the strength and viability of the kingdom.

I BELIEVE THIS PRINCIPLE MEANS:_____

TO APPLY THIS PRINCIPLE TO MY LIFE, I NEED TO:_____

_____

13. The Kingdom Taxation Principle: All kingdoms incorporate a taxation system, which allows its citizens to participate in the process of maintaining the kingdom infrastructure.

I BELIEVE THIS PRINCIPLE MEANS: _____

TO APPLY THIS PRINCIPLE TO MY LIFE, I NEED TO: _____

---

14. The Kingdom Army Principle: All kingdoms incorporate an army of security components to protect and defend their territory and citizens.

I BELIEVE THIS PRINCIPLE MEANS: _____

TO APPLY THIS PRINCIPLE TO MY LIFE, I NEED TO: _____

---

15. The Kingdom Delegated Authority Principle: All kingdoms establish a representative system that delegates responsibility to appointed citizens to serve as envoys or ambassadors of the kingdom or state.

I BELIEVE THIS PRINCIPLE MEANS: _____

TO APPLY THIS PRINCIPLE TO MY LIFE, I NEED TO: _____

---

16. The Kingdom Ambassador Principle: An ambassador speaks for the kingdom and does not represent himself, only his kingdom.

I BELIEVE THIS PRINCIPLE MEANS: _____

TO APPLY THIS PRINCIPLE TO MY LIFE, I NEED TO: _____

---

17. The Kingdom Education Principle: All kingdoms establish a system and program for training and educating its citizens.

I BELIEVE THIS PRINCIPLE MEANS: _____

TO APPLY THIS PRINCIPLE TO MY LIFE, I NEED TO: _____

---

18. The Kingdom Administration Principle: All kingdoms establish a system through which it administers its judgments and programs to the citizens.

I BELIEVE THIS PRINCIPLE MEANS: _____

TO APPLY THIS PRINCIPLE TO MY LIFE, I NEED TO: _____

(Quote From *Rediscovering the Kingdom*, Pages 219-223)

MEDITATION

"You were created to represent God and
His heavenly government through your
dominion over the territory of earth through
the gift you possess. May you rediscover your
true destiny through rediscovering your place
in the Kingdom of God as His representative
king-ruler over this colony called earth. You were
born to be born-again. It is your choice and your destiny!"
(*Rediscovering the Kingdom*, Page 227).

Pray that the Lord use the principles from this
lesson to help you rediscover your place in God's Kingdom.

UNDERSTANDING THE KINGDOM CONCEPTS—PART C

THIS IS TO MY FATHER'S GLORY, THAT YOU BEAR MUCH FRUIT, SHOWING YOURSELVES TO BE MY DISCIPLES.

(JOHN 15:8)

❖ Today's Devotion ❖

Here are the rest of the concepts and principles of kingdoms that you should know and become familiar with. Study and apply them to the message of the Kingdom of God and heaven taught by Jesus, in order to fully understand your purpose, potential, power, and position in life.

19. The Kingdom Principle of Glory: The glory of the king is all and everything in the kingdom that represents and manifests the true nature of the king himself.

I BELIEVE THIS PRINCIPLE MEANS: _____

TO APPLY THIS PRINCIPLE TO MY LIFE, I NEED TO:_____

_____

20. The Kingdom Principle of Worship: The worship of a king is the expression of the citizen's gratitude and appreciation to the king for his favor, privileges, and security of being in his kingdom.

I BELIEVE THIS PRINCIPLE MEANS: _____

TO APPLY THIS PRINCIPLE TO MY LIFE, I NEED TO:_____

_____

21. The Kingdom Principle of Provision: In all true kingdoms the king is obligated to provide for his citizens and thus he makes provisions at his own expense for their security and welfare.

I BELIEVE THIS PRINCIPLE MEANS: _____

TO APPLY THIS PRINCIPLE TO MY LIFE, I NEED TO:_____

_____

22. The Kingdom Principle of Influence: All kingdoms are committed to making the influence of the king and his will felt throughout the entire kingdom.

I BELIEVE THIS PRINCIPLE MEANS: _____

TO APPLY THIS PRINCIPLE TO MY LIFE, I NEED TO:_____

_____

23. The Kingdom Principle of Royal Favor: Royal favor is the sovereign prerogative of the king to extend a personal law to a citizen that positions that citizen to receive special privileges and advantages that are personally protected by the king.

I BELIEVE THIS PRINCIPLE MEANS: _____

TO APPLY THIS PRINCIPLE TO MY LIFE, I NEED TO: _____

---

24. The Kingdom Principle of Decree: A royal decree is a declaration of a king that becomes law to all. It is sustained by the king's personal commitment to bring the declaration or promise to pass.

I BELIEVE THIS PRINCIPLE MEANS: _____

TO APPLY THIS PRINCIPLE TO MY LIFE, I NEED TO: _____

---

25. The Kingdom Principle of Reputation: The king's reputation is important to the king and is the source of the glory of his name. A king's reputation is created and sustained by the conditions of his citizens and his kingdom. Therefore kings act in ways that are favorable to their name's sake.

I BELIEVE THIS PRINCIPLE MEANS: _____

TO APPLY THIS PRINCIPLE TO MY LIFE, I NEED TO: _____

---

26. The Kingdom Principle of Giving to a King: Giving to a king activates the king's obligation to demonstrate his glory and power to the giver and to prove that he is a greater king than all other kings. Giving to a king in his kingdom is the acknowledgment that all things belong to that king and the citizen is grateful. Because giving to a king is impossible (since all things already belong to the king), the act of giving benefits the citizen more than the king. Thus one should never come before a king empty-handed.

I BELIEVE THIS PRINCIPLE MEANS: _____

TO APPLY THIS PRINCIPLE TO MY LIFE, I NEED TO: _____

(Quote From *Rediscovering the Kingdom*, Pages 223-226)

MEDITATION

"From the above overview of kingdoms, one can see
that a kingdom is more advantageous than a republic.
Therefore it is more beneficial to be in a kingdom than
a democracy or any other form of government....
Welcome home to your dominion, and acknowledge
Him truly as King of the kings and Lord of the lords"
(*Rediscovering the Kingdom*, Page 226).

Pray "Thy Kingdom come" as you put
these principles into your daily walk in the Kingdom.

NOTES

NOTES

NOTES

NOTES

NOTES

NOTES

NOTES

NOTES

NOTES

NOTES

Additional copies of this book and other
book titles from DESTINY IMAGE are
available at your local bookstore.

For a complete list of our titles,
visit us at www.destinyimage.com
Send a request for a catalog to:

Destiny Image₍ₐ₎ Publishers, Inc.
P.O. Box 310
Shippensburg, PA 17257-0310

*"Speaking to the Purposes of God for This
Generation and for the Generations to Come"*